Bill Powell

On a clear day...

Clearview:
America's Course

First Edition

The Autobiography of William J. Powell

as told to and written by

Ellen Susanna Nösner

Foxsong

Published by Foxsong Publishing

Clearview:
America's Course

Published by Foxsong Publishing

Cover layout by Gary Bowden of Silk Design Company
Editing: Janeile Cannon
Photograph restoration, layout and editing: Crystalla
Page layout and editing: Susan Luzenski
Cover photograph of William J. Powell as appeared in People
Magazine: Donna Terek/People Weekly © 1996, Time Inc.

Foxsong Publishing
1769 Pine Creek Circle
Haslett, Michigan 48840
877-339-6918

ISBN 0-9677000-1-9

Library of Congress Control Number: 00-133049

Printed in the United States of America

Table of Contents

Preface

It was a cosmic twist of fate that led me to William J. Powell. I arrived at Clearview Golf Club on a cold, snowy day in November of 1996. My intent or so I thought, was to meet with his daughter and PGA/LPGA professional Renee Powell to plan a benefit golf tournament the following July.

Mr. Powell pulled up a chair and we began talking about shared interests like history, geography and Europe. We also talked about shared passions embracing different cultures, people and humanity. When it was time for me to leave I didn't want the day to end. As it turned out, God blessed me and that day was just the beginning.

I drove down the long lane from Clearview to US Highway 30 with tears flooding my eyes. I knew in my heart that William J. Powell would change my life forever. I would never be the same.

Mr. Powell's life, his love and his determination transformed me. His story of vision and passion is full of triumph and victory of the human spirit. It has a healing power that transcends understanding. That is truly his gift to you and me.

In the end, if I am asked, "What legacy do you pass on to future generations?"

I will smile and say, "I was the messenger."

January 17th, 2000
Ellen Susanna Nösner

Acknowledgements

Special heartfelt gratitude is extended to Mr. Powell and his family for their time and energy devoted to this book, including:

Renee Powell
Lawrence Powell
Mary Alice Walker
Rose Marie Mathews

Very special acknowledgement to Marcella Powell and her loving spirit.

The following have lent expertise to this project:

Joe Louis Barrow Jr., Executive Director,
    The First Tee
Euley Glenn
Edie Jones, Ph.D
Scott Kauffman, Golfweek staff writer
Norma Marcere, Ph.D
Bill Tijerina, photographer
Paul Shankle, Stark County Engineers
W. Michael Sherman, Ph.D

Ellen Susanna Nösner
May 2000

Foreword From...

The only African-American woman who is a class A golfer in the Ladies Professional Golf Association (LPGA) and the only black female, also class A, in the 26,000 member Professional Golf Association (PGA) of America.

It is very rare that we are fortunate enough to come in contact with an individual whose life has had an impact on past and present generations, and will have an even greater impact on the future.

As William J. Powell shares his trials and triumphs with us in his autobiography, *Clearview: America's Course,* we are inspired and given hope that dreams can come true, if we are willing to stay the course.

This is the story of an American hero who believed that in America anything was possible, and set out to prove just that.

Throughout his entire journey in life he faced obstacles that could have caused him to react in a negative manner. Instead, he chose to react in a positive nature and by moving the "c" in reaction, Clearview Golf Course became his "creation," a creation that runs deep in the veins of his entire family.

He has inspired each of us to strive for greater heights, to never give up, to find a way over, under or around whatever obstacles confront us. Finally he passed on to us that pride and integrity are something no one can take away from you.

You will not only want to read each word of this very moving book, but also to reflect on its many messages.

I am so honored to have the opportunity to share a few words in this foreword because for my entire life, I have been fortunate to be able to call him "Daddy."

Renee Powell,
Daughter and Clearview Club Pro

Introduction

More than 50 years ago, Bill Powell set out upon a mission that many thought was impossible: an African American with limited funds designing and building his own golf course, using only the physical strength and mental tenacity that God had bestowed upon him.

Strength is the cornerstone of the Powell legacy. Bill Powell was blessed with the mental fortitude and wherewithal to endure the hardships facing people of color for the better part of the 20th century. He was good enough to fight for his country overseas in World War II, but he was not good enough to play many of America's golf courses upon his return to civilian life.

After building Clearview Golf Course in East Canton, Ohio, he was rebuffed from PGA membership as a result of his race. Yet the resilient Powell would not allow his spirit to bow to matters not in his control. Eventually he would be elected into PGA membership, and today his race and dignity are hallmarks of his legendary career.

Clearview is a living testament to Bill Powell. The historic facility reflects what one person can accomplish through dedication and persistence. Indeed, Bill Powell is the epitome of African American entrepreneurship.

Bill Powell is a man who overcame the longest odds to make his mark in golf. Generations of future golfers will be the beneficiary of his dedication and devotion to the game of golf. I feel blessed having had the opportunity to share a small part of his amazing life. I also am thankful he has allowed me to feel like a part of his family.

Jim L. Awtrey
Chief Executive Officer
The PGA of America

Dedication

I dedicate this book to all my friends who have been at my side throughout the years at Clearview and to the loyal boosters that have supported Clearview from its birth in 1946; to my dear deceased partner and wife Marcella, to my son William B. who contributed in his best and most sincere way; to Nathan Martin; brothers Berry and Dempsey who did their part; to Ralph Petros who was my very best and dearest friend; and may God forgive me for leaving the other dear friends out of print. You are on my mind.

William J. Powell

Chapter One: Determined Beginnings

....but let justice roll down like water, and
righteousness like an ever-flowing stream.

Amos 5:24

From the very beginning, I wanted to believe it was possible to feel justice. I did not. I knew in my heart that righteousness should be like an ever-flowing stream. It wasn't. That is why determination has fueled the fire of the decisions that have shaped my life.

My life has also been filled with a struggle of give and take. Either somebody didn't want to give me what I deserved or somebody was trying to take it away - - but not my pride or integrity. I had both. I was taught integrity and possessed pride passed to me from my parents and family. I wasn't about to let anyone take that away from me. After all, once your pride and integrity are gone your dreams are next. Everything was at stake and I was determined to hold onto my dreams.

That's how it all started - - Clearview Golf Club in East Canton, Ohio. Can you believe it? Fifty-four years later, and I'm still the only black man in America to design, build and operate his own golf course. It wasn't easy and of course there were sacrifices. It took hard work day in and day out, year after year. First came nine holes, then eighteen and everything in between. This is my story, the story of a man in America who refused to be beaten down. One man who was not willing to beg to play golf just because his only handicap was the color of his skin. Now Clearview is my course... and it's America's course.

When I returned to Canton after World War II (WWII), I realized playing at a private club was totally out of the question. When I was turned away from public courses as well, I'd had enough.

It was at that defining moment I decided, "I'll just build my own."

I was driven by a dream. I refused to be daunted. I rose above prejudice while holding onto hope and surviving on the love of my family. I had to do what I knew I could do... what I must do... what I did do.

For me, it began November 22, 1916 in Butler County, Greenville, Alabama. I was the third child of six children, three boys and three girls. I had two older brothers, Dempsey and Berry. My twin sisters, Mary Alice and Rose Marie came along nine years later, then Vivien and my baby brother Roy. Roy died shortly after he was born.

My parents, Berry and Massaleaner, were born in Butler County, Alabama too. My paternal grandparents, Mary and Frank, whom I remember as a three-year-old, were also from Butler County. My mother's parents, Albert and Julia Simpson, moved to Detroit from Alabama when I was very young. A slave owner fathered my paternal grandfather, Great-Grandpa Tite. The slave owner claimed him as his own and wanted to educate him but Great-Grandpa Tite was a rebel by family accounts and wanted to live only with his mother and the rest of his family. So he denounced the slave owner's claim and spurned the offer.

The history and heritage of my family is very important because they are the backbone of who I am. My parents were exceptional human beings who modeled characteristics profiled in the very best of us. My father was a deep thinker with a clear thought process. He was creative, fiercely tenacious, and determined. Thriftiness was crucial to him and there was no question about confidence. He and my mother both gave me the gift of mental cleansing. I would watch my father, night after night, sit quietly and read the Bible in private.

My mother shared several characteristics with my father... tenacity and confidence. Mother also possessed a strong sense of aggressiveness and pride.

She never stopped saying, "Willie, people can take away anything but your pride."

Times were very tough in the south for lots of people during World War I (WWI) in 1916. Jobs were scarce and good ones didn't get around to blacks. My father, industrious and entrepreneurial, owned a general store but during the war things just dried up. There's a lot of pride in working. By 1919, WWI had just ended. So for those "colored" people who thirsted to provide a better future for themselves and their families they had little choice but to uproot their loved ones and migrate from the cotton fields of the South to the factories of the North. At that time those of African American descent were referred to as colored.

My father had heard there was work in the pottery factories and brickyards in a place called Minerva, Ohio. Uncle Joe and Aunt Ida had already moved to this small northeastern village of Minerva. Staying was not an option so my father packed us up and north we headed toward a new life and steady work.

Minerva was a rather prosperous little village with a portion of the land lying on the southeastern corner of Stark County and the remainder in Carroll County. Today, three counties share Minerva's property, including Columbiana. At one time it also had three railroads passing through town: the Wheeling-Lake Erie, New York Central and the Pennsylvania. Each had passenger stations.

Minerva was laid out in 1835 so by 1919 it was certainly a mature village. Originally, the black population in Minerva started because the village had a pottery factory that fired the big kilns with coal. It was hard dirty work firing the kilns with tons of coal and breaking up the clinkers, and then raking out the ashes. No one ever complained. Eventually, the pottery factory closed down. Because it was so difficult for blacks to purchase property in what was an all white town, they began to move out. We were the only permanent black family with kids who lived there.

Fortunately my father had a friend in town, an American Railway Express agent, who helped him locate a lot on the west edge of town in an area known as Oklahoma. Because he believed it was a good place to raise a family he purchased the land and built a house. He was a physically slight man but could and did do anything he had to do. He did carpentry work and built his own furniture. He built the kitchen cabinets and did all of the cement work. In fact, my sister Rose lives in the house that my father built where I grew up at 213 Pennsylvania Avenue. My father was quite a man.

A determined man who gave me my determined beginnings.

Folks in Minerva were friendly to us. We were fortunate to grow up in a small, rural town. By this time, we were in the 1920s and times were tough for everyone. So there was a spirit of camaraderie between the townspeople of Minerva that embraced us. One thing was certain, no one had anything and no one was jealous. We were all in the same boat and it seemed as if it was sinking. Prosperity was not right around the corner as President Hoover claimed. In fact, what was right around the corner was the Great Depression; prosperity was going the other way.

As children, we spent most of our time playing outdoors on the playground. My brother Berry and I were very close. He was two years older than me. We also played with other neighborhood kids in Minerva.

I have always loved nature and I spent a lot of my time playing in the woods becoming a survival expert. I could pick out an edible mushroom in the dark.

By the time I was 10 my love for sports had taken over. If I wasn't on the golf course I was playing tennis at the courts American Electric Switch had built, or playing baseball on the diamond at Minerva Wax Paper. You could also find me playing football on what was our grade school football field, St. Gabriel's parking lot. We didn't have any goal posts but it was a great practice field.

Sports have always provided valuable lessons for me; discipline, competitive spirit and determination. You, not someone else, step up to the ladder and climb. It is up to the individual to make his own climb.

Golf is a perfect example. Golf is also a good model for life... the more you put in, the more you get.

Then came the Dolphie Roam episode. One day I got into a scrape with Dolphie, and his father came along and grabbed me while egging Dolphie on to kick me. I was just a little kid and terrified. I remember telling Dolphie that his daddy wasn't always going to be around and he better think twice before he kicked me. What happened next was a lesson about uneven playing fields. Dolphie's father became very angry and he threatened to kick me himself. Finally he let go of me and I ran home crying to my mother. Mrs. Gurney, our next-door neighbor was visiting when I came running home. Mr. and Mrs. Gurney lived at 103 Pennsylvania. When I told my mother and Mrs. Gurney what happened Mrs. Gurney became livid. She was a small lady with a real temper. Her husband was an engineer on the New York Central Railroad so they were a substantial and influential family in town. Mrs. Gurney then proceeded to march right down to Dolphie's house with sparks flying out of her hair and took on Dolphie Roam's daddy. It meant a lot to my family and me that she took on such a bully alone and defended us.

We had hoped that moving up north to Ohio would mean leaving the Klan behind. But it didn't. I suppose that is why so many blacks coming up from the south didn't stop until they got to Canada. One Klan memory is etched indelibly in my mind. Shortly after my baby brother Roy was born, he got pneumonia and was very ill. One night, fighting for his life, the Klan was on a nearby hill less than 200 yards away burning a cross and shooting off cannons. This night of terror was different. We had become accustomed to the Klan shooting off their guns incessantly but never cannons. They were coming in very close. That pushed one of our neighbors over the edge.

Mr. Knox wasn't going to stand for what the Klan was doing. He was a white man, who like many folks in Minerva, came from Tennessee stock. Mr. Knox lived a few houses down from us on Pennsylvania near Mrs. Gurney. Mr. Knox got his gun, marched up the hill and had a standoff with the Klan. He was point blank about the situation.

He told them, "Those folks down there have a sick baby and I'll leave the whole bunch of you laying up here if you don't keep quiet."

Thankfully they left and let my baby brother die in peace. It took a lot of courage for Mr. Knox to do that for us. My experience has been, sometimes the good comes with the bad in this life. You may have to look for it, but it's there.

We all have defining moments in our lives, as children and adults. Times when we can take one path or another. Times when we must make a choice and hope it is the right one. Situations present themselves and change our lives forever. One of mine happened in the schoolyard of Minerva Grade School when I was 12 years old in the sixth grade.

Mr. R. R. Vaughn was our grade school principal. All of us kids were outside in the schoolyard lined up for a fire drill. Mr. Vaughn, for no particular reason, changed my life. He said something to me that became a source of motivation and a yardstick by which to measure myself from that point on.

He got real serious and looked me in the eye and said, "Billy, you know you are a little colored boy and you have to realize you can't do things just as good as a white boy - - you have to do them better!"

As I listened, I was shocked that he would be so honest with a colored kid. It was a brutal adult statement to a young child, a very impressionable child. Little did he know that what he said became imprinted in my mind. It still is... and it's etched on my heart. His words became a very important tool for my life and became the under-pinning for every step I took. His words also helped create my determination to be better than the best. From that point on I became my own role model and raised my own bar.

Setting and raising my own bar would prove to be beneficial, especially since three years earlier, at the age of nine, I had discovered the sport that would impact and change my life forever - - golf.

Willie on the steps of Minerva School (1923)

"Doing things better in the second grade"

Chapter Two: Potential And Passion

"Tell me not, in mournful numbers,
Life is but an empty dream!
- - For the soul is dead that slumbers,
And things are not what they seem." [1]

From A Psalm of Life by Henry Wadsworth Longfellow

My first introduction to golf came in a kind of roundabout way. My friend, George Tomlinson, was a neighborhood playmate and just as adventurous as I was. One day, George's father told him that a golf course was being built about seven miles west of town. Now, I didn't know what a golf course was, but I was always a curious person and it was a nice day for a walk. The straightest route to the course was through a railway spur that was connected to the main line of the New York Central Railroad. The rail line ran through a tunnel-cut which had been a tunnel until the top collapsed. The railroad cleared the debris but the cut was very narrow. This made it a dangerous place to be when the old steam locomotives came roaring through. No matter, we were headed straight for the course.

When we finally reached Edgewater Golf Course it was like a whole new world opening up right before my very eyes. I had never seen anything so beautiful. The course wasn't nearly as manicured like Augusta National is today, but the tees and greens, the streams and sand bunkers fascinated me. While I didn't understand anything about the game yet, just watching the golfers hit the ball so high and far into the air simply amazed me. I couldn't understand how they did it and I couldn't wait to try it myself.

We also feasted our eyes on a steel wheel Model T Ford that had been converted into a tractor and was used to mow the fairways. This vehicle had a Model T chassis and twelve-inch-wide steel rear wheels attached to a chain drive with three-quarter-inch flat metal studs. It was a rather odd looking contraption, but then, this was two years before the Model A came out. Fascinated by the golf course and the sport itself, the day just disappeared. Naturally, being kids we completely lost track of time and pretty soon it was getting dark. We made our way back down to the railroad track, hiking seven miles and dodging trains. By the time I reached my house I was hoping, perhaps even praying, that my mother was asleep. I walked up the steps quiet as a church mouse and I gently turned the doorknob. Mother, who had no idea of where I'd been, was worried sick. She was not only waiting for me, but about as angry as I'd ever seen her in all my nine years. I knew what was coming next. She sent me out in the yard and told me to get a nice whippy switch from one of the willows in the front yard. When I came back in, I got one of the worst whippings of my life. It was all the worse because I had to fetch the switch myself. I knew I deserved it but I also knew that right then and there I'd be going back to that golf course. I was hooked. Little did I know at the time that one day, I'd be designing and building my own golf course.

Pretty soon my brother Berry and I were caddying every chance we could. I don't think my parents were thrilled about their little Willie working at such an early age, but in those days when the chance came along to make some money and help out the family, you took it. The little bit of money we earned helped us to buy our own clothes. That may not sound like much today but it meant everything to us back then.

Berry and I were the only black caddies and we took our mother's lessons to heart. She always told us we should be proud of our color. But because we were black we had to work twice as hard and be twice as good as the white kids. Principal Vaughn taught me that lesson.

Berry and I worked hard. Our pay was 35 cents a bag and we always tried to carry doubles. Even if it meant we might be lagging behind late in the day, especially on those days when you could get two loops, or go out twice. It was a good feeling to come home with $1.40 in my pocket and see the look on my parent's faces. Soon Berry and I became Class "A" caddies and the better players started asking for us. That meant the rounds were shorter because we spent less time looking for lost balls. More importantly, it meant we had the opportunity to study good players and mimic them. I still think that's the best way for kids to learn a sport especially one as difficult as golf. You learn by example, don't you?

The fact that Berry and I were willing to work hard and were so interested in the game caught the attention of the caddy master, Glen Lautzenheiser. He wasn't just the caddy master; he did just about everything else at Edgewater too. He was the greens keeper and did a lot of the maintenance work around the course.

When we didn't have a loop we'd do things like picking weeds, helping fertilize the course and repair golf clubs. You name it we did it. Along the way we got a full education about the entire game. I loved every minute of it. I could feel deep inside I was born for golf.

Golf was a little different during the 1920s and '30s. The golfer had full sets of clubs but all the shafts were hickory wood, which made them somewhat lighter. The bags were made of leather and whenever they got wet, it made them somewhat heavier. In addition, the straps on the golf bags were only about an inch wide and most had no padding as they do today.

Even the tees (pegs) were different. Some were celluloid tees, wood rite-hite tees, rubber tees and pressed cardboard tees. A water bucket and sand could also be available at each tee so that golfers could make their own tees if they so desired. To make your own tees you just took a pinch of sand and placed it on the ground. If the sand got dry you would simply mix a little water with the sand to give it moisture for firmness.

A number eight iron was used as the pitching iron since wedges were not yet invented. So, if you had a bunker or trap shot you would simply lay open the face of the eight or nine iron and cut the shot.

The first steel shaft I remember seeing was a Hagen iron with Bristol steel. Later, the Croydon club came out with a shaft they called the torsion shaft, but a lot of the golfers referred to it as the torture shaft. Back in those days, Croydon was one of the top club lines, but I thought MacGregor really had the best woods and Spaulding had the best irons at that time. Bobby Jones made the Spaulding name great. He had won the

Grand Slam of Golf and everyone wanted a set of Bobby Jones Clubs made by Spaulding.

In the '20s you would always find a lot of clubs broken because of the wooden shafts. Today, however, you may often find a broken shaft around a large piece of wood, better known as a tree. Toward the '30s I began to see steel-shafted clubs at the course. My very first club was a wood shaft Burkey-built driver. My first steel shafts were by MacGregor, a ladies driver and brassy.

At this time, my mother was doing day work for Dr. Casey who was a general physician in Minerva. Sometimes I would go along with her to Dr. Casey's house. He lived at 206 Main Street. She always insisted I be clean, neat, and well behaved. Dr. Casey began to take a liking to me. He was quite a character too. He'd been a captain in the Army during WWI and was now in his 40s or early 50s.

I remember a few funny things about him. He was a lefty, which was rare for golfers back then and he always had a stogie in his mouth. He never lit it, but it was always there. The other funny thing was we could never just say yes to him, it was always a loud "Yes sir!" - - just like in the movies. When Doc Casey found out I had a burning desire to learn and play the sport, he took me out to the golf course and I became Dr. Casey's playing partner every weekday right at noon. That's right, I said golf with him, not caddy. Bud Myers was Doc Casey's caddy, a cousin of the course's owner. I'd meet Doc Casey at his house at noon and off we'd go to the newly opened Edgewater Golf Course. He was the most predictable man I've ever known. We'd play nine holes every weekday during the summer, never more and rarely less. He never played on weekends and I never saw him hit a putt shorter than three feet. He'd just scrape it towards the hole and give it to himself. I've often thought it funny that I never caddied for him. We never talked much on the course and I don't remember him ever giving me a lesson.

Dr. Casey gets the credit for encouraging me, my game, and giving me the opportunity to actually play golf on a daily basis. In those days, it was pretty remarkable for a white man to do something like that for a little black boy. I realize I was lucky, and I know I have Dr. Casey to thank for opening the door to golf for me.

My golf game improved pretty quickly. No amount of effort will equal ability but if you have ability, effort goes a long way in separating you from the rest of the crowd. Remember eagles do not flock they fly alone.

When I got to high school I was the captain of the football team. I had always wanted to play football. I wanted to play so bad that when I was little I would put my sneakers inside my older brother Dempsey's football shoes. He was the captain of the football team his senior year in 1930. When it was my turn to play football I would practice a lot in our backyard and my twin sisters Mary Alice and Rose Marie would run after the football to retrieve it for me until they could run no more. My practicing paid off when I became the captain of the Minerva High School football team - - the only black kid in the class.

My friends and I also formed a golf team. The athletic director of Minerva High School, Jim McBride, asked me to be the captain and coach of the golf team. We played matches against other local schools on different courses in the area. Canton McKinley had a golf team and so did Alliance High School and Wooster. Dick Kutsch, Ralph Petros, Walter Lyle and I were the golf team. We remained friends during our lifetime. Ralph and I were the best of friends until his death a few years ago. I'm the only one left now.

One of my jobs as coach was to schedule the golf matches, that proved a little difficult because of the lack of high school teams, only three in the area. It became very competitive. Those were tough matches and my game really moved up a notch with the competition. In order to be really good you have to believe you are really good and believe you are the best. I believed I could hold my own in the local junior tournaments. In fact, I was pretty sure I could win - - if I could get a chance to play at Orchard Hills.

My first experience in a real junior tournament proved to be the experience of a lifetime. It took place at Orchard Hills Country Club, which today is Arrowhead Country Club. Orchard Hills was a pretty fancy private club in North Canton. Frank Deems had organized a tournament and I was determined to play. Fact is, the people running these tournaments didn't really want black kids playing and they especially didn't want one of us to win. I'll tell you exactly what it was like.

Some of the folks around Minerva encouraged me to play. So I decided to give it a try. We didn't have a car, so I hitchhiked 21 miles one way with my bag and clubs over my back, not knowing exactly where the course was. I didn't even know if I'd get a ride or be on time. When I got there, Mr. Deems and the others didn't know what to do with me. I stood around for two hours waiting for them to decide if I could play in their tournament. They didn't want me to play, but on the other hand they knew I was a good player and popular in the area. I was also well known because I had caddied for many of the members over the previous seven years. They didn't want to cause a stir by keeping me out but that didn't automatically get me in either. They finally decided to let me play. Imagine how I felt. I suppose I should have been upset to be treated that way but I was so elated to finally get a chance to play that I didn't have the time or emotion to get upset. Sadly, even though I was only 16, I was already conditioned to being mistreated. I don't think anyone learns to accept that kind of mistreatment but to survive you do get used to it.

The tournament was an 18-hole qualifying round the first day and I played with a kid by the name of Army Armagita. His sisters followed us around and when I started to really play good they began rooting for me. Henry Hein, a member at Orchard Hills who I had caddied for at Edgewater also came out to follow us and before I knew it I had a fine little gallery for myself. That must have given me a boost because I went out and shot the lowest qualifying score. Then I hitchhiked home 21 miles.

The next morning I hitchhiked back 21 miles to Orchard Hills Country Club. The three lowest scores were supposed to play in the finals, but instead of playing just three they decided to play six. Although my score was the lowest they decided to place me in the three-

some with the two highest scores. The tournament consisted of 36 holes, 18 in the morning and 18 in the
afternoon. On the morning round I once again shot the
best score and now the tournament officials were forced
to place me in the group with the two lowest scores. I
can't prove it but I suspect Mr. Deems and the rest of
them were hoping that, by not pairing me evenly with
my closest competitors, they would throw my game
off and eliminate me. I know a lot of other people thought
that's why they did it. I still shot the best score. Now
they didn't have any choice but to make the proper
pairings for the final round that afternoon, which is
the position I should have held from the very beginning.

I went out to tee off after lunch and was surprised
to find the biggest gallery that had ever watched me
play. It didn't make me nervous to have all those people
pulling for me. I just went out calm as could be and
played my game. Everything went fine until the fifteenth
hole. It was a par five. I was leading the tournament
when I hit my second shot into a peach orchard. I was
in a roadway and got a free drop. I had to hit the ball
up over a barn - - no small feat. So I opened up my
niblick, a 9 iron today, threw open the blade, and hit
the sweetest little cut shot you ever saw. Folks were
going wild. The ball cleared the barn and was heading
straight for the pin but it nicked a narrow limb of a
huge maple tree on the way down and came to rest
knee-deep in Timothy rough. I tried to hack at it a couple
times but by the time I was finished I'd taken an eight,
lost my lead and was completely shaken. Remember,
I was only 16. It was the first time my nerves got to me

on the course and I didn't know how to react. I was so nervous my hands could barely hold the grip of the club because of the sweat. As I walked to the next tee, the club pro, Walt Ingram, noticed I was visibly shaken. He asked me if I wanted anything to drink. He brought me a cup of orange juice but I was so nervous and my hands were shaking so badly I couldn't even hold the cup. How was I going to hit the ball?

I wanted to win so bad I could actually taste it. I had a burning desire to prove to those tournament officials who sought to keep me from playing, that I was best. I was so distraught I just wanted to turn and walk away and out of the tournament but I knew that was wrong and people would call me a quitter. After completing the final three holes, I finished in third place. I left quietly hitchhiking 21of the longest miles of my life back home.

There I was...16 and devastated but not willing to give up. I truly believed I could win. I wanted to be a champion that day. I had the heart of a champion but there were more days to follow. At that moment I had no idea how far away victory really was. So, I would seek and eventually find peace of mind on a course where the only color that mattered was the greens- - my greens, my course, Clearview.

I went on to college and things improved, at least for a while. I was excited about going to college at Wilberforce. Wilberforce University is in Xenia, Ohio. I attended with my brother Berry. Wilberforce was an all black university and I enjoyed it. I was a member of the Wilberforce's Green Wave football team. I was a member of the golf team too and one of my fondest memories was our golf team making a little bit of sports history.

In 1937, our team traveled to Ada to play the team from Ohio Northern University at Lost Creek Country Club in Lima, Ohio. Our foursome was awesome. My brother Berry, Howard Broadus from Steubenville, Earl Galloway from Woodbury, New Jersey and I were history in the making. It was the first inter-racial collegiate golf match in America and I'm proud to say we came away winners. We won again when the guys from Ohio Northern University came to Dayton for a rematch. I was so proud and full of promise.

I soon became increasingly and continually fatigued. I was diagnosed with an enlarged heart. I left college and came home to heal myself through a self-cure of exercise. This condition was diagnosed before the draft and I still ended up enlisted.

Was I good enough to make it on Tour? I had the potential and believe me I had the passion. Opportunity was not part of the equation. I will never know the answer to that question. What I do know is I never had the chance to find out. Golf isn't a game you can put down and pick back up. If you are going to be good you have to be able to practice and compete against the best. I was never allowed to try. Today, that still hurts. I was confident- -full of hope and over-flowing with potential and passion.

Favorite caddies, William and Berry (1928)

Taking a swing, age 22

Chapter Three: Till Death Us Do Part

"That love is all there is, is all we know of love." [2]
Emily Dickinson

Sunsets and sunrises, fifty-six contented and soulful years with my wife Marcella is something for which I am very grateful. Our marriage and the foundation of our relationship were bedrock. Having Marcella by my side, and willing to try anything I wanted to pursue, is part of the miracle of Clearview. Here's exactly how our meeting and life together unfolded.

After my college days, I worked a variety of jobs. For a time I sold fish door-to-door. I also sold Armstrong suits and Knapp shoes. My oldest brother Dempsey and I even went around washing cars. The 1930s were much worse than the 1920s and you had to do whatever you could to earn a dollar. Times were just that tough.

Just when I thought my luck would never change, Lady Luck finally began to smile down on me.

There was a big 4th of July picnic at Jackson Park in Canton. My brother Berry was going with a girl he was seeing regularly and they invited me to tag along. When we arrived at the park, Berry's girlfriend, Lorene Strictland, spotted her best friend on the tennis court. Her name was Marcella Oliver.

What I didn't know was in earlier conversations Marcella had asked my brother Berry if he had a younger brother. So the pump was already primed so to speak. We hit it off from the very beginning - - "just one look" as the line from the song goes. In retrospect, I suspect that our meeting wasn't all chance but perhaps more a case of fate. Of course, there's no accounting for what Lady Luck will do.

That 4th of July was another defining moment for me. That night a dance was planned after the picnic and Marcella asked me if I'd like to go with her and some friends. I said yes, of course, and from that point on we were together always. Marcella was my best friend, my wife, the mother of our three children, and my true partner in Clearview for all the years to come. She was not only the most right thing that had ever happened to me, she was the best thing that ever happened and perhaps the most important reason for Clearview becoming a reality.

Marcella Oliver was born on April 20, 1917 in Alliance, Ohio, but as a toddler her family moved to the big city of Canton.

Marcella was a gentle soul and possessed a generous spirit. She was very focused, always supportive and intelligent, with such a lovable personality. She was all that and more, especially her sincere and genuine nature. She was the most authentic person I've ever known. She passed from this life to the next on June 9, 1996.

The poet Kahlil Gibran speaks of marriage as, "Two people doing together what neither one can do alone."[3]

This was certainly the case with Marcella and me. When I met Marcella and during our courtship, Marcella was living with Dr. Norma Marcere and her husband in Canton. Her mother had passed on from tuberculosis while she was in high school. She was the oldest child of eight and for a year before her mother died she would save her lunch money to visit her mother in the Molly Stark Tuberculosis Sanitarium. Tragically, after her mother died, the family wasn't able to stay together. Most of the family scattered and Marcella moved in as a foster child with Dr. Marcere and her husband Percy. Dr. Marcere's mother, Ida Snipes, had been a friend of Marcella's mother, Hattie Oliver. It wasn't long before she was part of the entire Marcere family, including Dr. Marcere's two younger children Norma Jean and Al, short for Alluren.

Marcella flew under Dr. Marcere's wing when she was studying drama at the Urban League. Marcella was quiet, but stood out because she always tried to do her very best at everything. She was extremely kind, cooperative, and willing to do anything, according to Dr. Marcere. That was not only true of her efforts in drama class but life as well. She also possessed a deep faith and a sense of connection with the divine.

Marcella finished high school and dreamed of being a nurse. She applied for admission at the Nurses Training Center at Mercy Hospital but was denied admission because of her color. She was told she would have to go to St. Louis if she wanted to attend nursing school. I don't think she ever really recovered from that setback. Extinguished dreams are indeed tragic.

At least she didn't feel she was alone or that she was the only person who had experienced this kind of educational racism. Dr. Marcere had teaching credentials for 30 years before she was allowed to teach, because of her color. In fact, when she finally was allowed to teach, she taught school in Massillon and Akron, never in her own hometown. First, they told her she didn't have enough education. The same teaching credentials however guaranteed white teachers a job. And after she earned a Ph.D. she was told she had too much education. Marcella witnessed all of this while living with Dr. Marcere and her family.

After our 4th of July meeting we were married on November 22, 1940, my birthday, in St. Peter's Church in downtown Canton. St. Peter's is the second oldest Catholic Church in Canton. It was founded in 1845 as a German Catholic Church and it is a beautiful cathedral graced with mosaic tile throughout the entire church.

On bended-knee, at the side altar on the south side of the main altar is where Father Heimann officiated as we took our vows. Three chairs, now covered in light sea foam velvet are located immediately behind the kneeling altar. This was the designated area for weddings if you were not Catholic or a member of the church.

We had no money. Dr. Marcere arranged for our wedding reception at the Phyllis Wheatley, which was similar to the YWCA, only for blacks since we weren't allowed at the Canton Y.

We had no honeymoon. We began and ended our lives together on love. We were so poor when we first got married we couldn't even afford our own apartment, so as newlyweds we spent over a month living apart, Marcella with Dr. Marcere and I with my parents in Minerva, 16 miles east of Canton.

It was hard finding a decent place to live in those days and we were very lucky to find Mrs. Williams on Lippert Road. She rented us one room with full access to her entire house. She was a single mother with a boy named Elgee that everyone called Junior. She was a wonderful woman and we lived there even after our first son Billie was born June 16, 1941.

Our next move was to an apartment on Eighth Street and we were living there when I was drafted into WWII. My brother Dempsey and his wife Lorina occupied the upstairs apartment with us on Eighth Street.

When I first met Marcella I had a steady job at National Brickyard but it was miserable work. After we were married I knew I had to find a better line of work. At that time, the Timken Company, a roller bearing and steel manufacturer, was running ads in newspapers in West Virginia and Kentucky for laborers. They were desperately short of workers but they wouldn't even consider hiring a black man, no matter how badly they needed workers. They wouldn't even let a black man wait in the employment line. The police would tell you there was nothing for you here and to move on.

Back in those days there wasn't anything lower than a black man, but I never forgot my mother's lesson; always be proud of myself. She knew life wouldn't be easy for any of her children.

I still remember her saying, "You don't have to brag on yourself, just carry yourself well and people will take notice."

In the '40s there were only five types of jobs for a black man. It didn't matter whether you had a college degree. The jobs were: chauffeur, yardman, Pullman porter, doctor or dentist. There weren't many black doctors or dentists either. In fact, at that time there were only three black doctors in Canton. There was a huge gap between professional blacks and general laborers but we were all very close, because the whites certainly weren't socializing with us. All we had were each other.

I never gave up. Never. I went back to Timken day after day. I told the Employment Manager he had to hire me because I had a family to support. I even got a letter of recommendation from the County Prosecutor, Frenchie Bartholemeh. I had caddied for him at Edgewater and he was happy to help me out.

Finally, they hired me as a custodian to clean up a new building that had just been completed. I kept my mouth shut and did whatever needed to be done. It was a dirty job. Worse than that it was a dead end job. It was going nowhere and in those days you couldn't transfer from department to department. So when I heard that Hercules Motor was hiring blacks I went to talk to them and then I went to see Mr. Greene at Timken. At the same time I was doing landscape work on the side for Mr. Greene who was the head of personnel. After I talked to Mr. Greene, I went to Bob Parks, Director of Personnel and told him I had a chance to work at Hercules. He wrote me a full-page letter of recommendation and off I went to start my new job at Hercules.

Well, we've all heard the phrase "the grass is always greener on the other side." I was now right in the middle of that situation. It was horrible. At the end of a day at Hercules I had enough oil on me to change the oil in a car! It was even dirtier than my custodian work at Timken. Meanwhile, I was still doing landscaping work for Mr. Greene.

One day Mrs. Greene asked, "How do you like your new job?"

My reply was, "I don't! I might as well have stayed at Timken."

Before I could blink my eyes I was back at Timken at the Savannah Avenue plant working on a turret lathe. I didn't even have to give 2 weeks notice at Hercules because Timken owned part of Hercules. Finally, I had a job that was challenging and not so dirty. I had to grind my own tools and set the machines on diameter for 35-mm shot.

My next assignment was in back of the boiler house where I ran the scales. It was here that I got the toughest assignment of my entire life. Mr. Greene wanted me to recruit two other people of color that would be as dependable as I, whom I could recommend for a job. In other words, he wanted me to find duplicates of myself. The problem was someone like that already had a job or already was in line for one. I searched and I searched, no luck. I finally found one man for the job. His name was Ernie Edwards from Massillon, he was a former all-state basketball player and he was washing cars. I never did find number two.

Then one day after I got off work the Timken Police Sergeant said to me, "The Chief wants you to come down tomorrow to get fitted for a policeman's uniform."

"Don't be playing with me," I said.

In those days, in Canton, it was unheard of for a black man to be on the police/security force for Timken.

Like any place, Timken had its faults. They thought they owned you body and soul. However, if you had a legitimate gripe you could go right on in and see the president of the company. It didn't matter if you were black or white.

When WWII broke out, they promised us that if we went into the service, we'd have our jobs waiting for us when we came out. They kept their word and I stayed at Timken for 23 years.

One Sunday afternoon late in 1941, I said good-bye to Marcella and Billy about 2:30 p.m. and headed to work in my '39 Ford. It was a Sunday but that didn't mean I had the day off. The war was raging in both Europe and the Pacific and Timken was running shifts seven days a week. Timken played a major part in the manufacturing of tapered roller bearings and steel. How they were used made them important to the war effort --the war rolled on Timken products.

It was a warm and rather sunny day for early December. I remember it being just a beautiful day. Suddenly a news flash came on the radio. The Japanese had attacked our bases at Pearl Harbor in Hawaii. The details were sketchy at that point but there was no doubt about it...we were going to war.

I don't suppose it should have been a surprise to anyone with half a wit. We'd been following the war news in all the papers. Despite what the politicians said folks mostly figured it was just a matter of time before we got into the fight. Still, I don't think anyone expected anything as dramatic as Pearl Harbor.

My first reaction was shock. I just couldn't believe the Japanese were crazy enough to attack us like that. What were they thinking? I thought the war with Japan would be over in a week. How in the world did a little island country think they could beat us? Most of the guys at work felt the same way. We thought we could handle the Japanese pretty easily. The

Nazis would be a different story.

When I got home from work that night I told Marcella I didn't think I'd be drafted. I wasn't just trying to make her feel better. That's what I honestly believed. I figured that I'd be exempt from the draft because of my security job. I also thought that since my older brothers, Dempsey and Berry, were already in the service my chances of being called up were pretty slim. I didn't think the government would take all three boys from one family.

There was one other thing I figured I had going for me - - in a rather odd way. I didn't think they wanted any blacks in the service. After all, in 1938 and 1939 when the Depression was so bad, my brother Dempsey tried to enlist and was turned down. There was no need for colored troops back then. I was wrong on every count. Uncle Sam said, "I want you," and he got me.

Once I was drafted things moved rather quickly. I went to Columbus to be inducted into the Army and within a week or so I was headed for a brief stop at Columbia, South Carolina Army Air Base and then to my first posting, the Army Air Corps base at Anderson Field in Walterboro, South Carolina.

It is ironic that I went to Columbus to be inducted into the Army in 1942 and returned to Columbus to be inducted into the Ohio Veterans Hall of Fame in November 1998. In 1999, the Governor of Ohio appointed me to the Ohio Veterans Hall of Fame selection committee.

Everyone was worried about husbands, fathers, and brothers going to war but if Marcella was worried, she didn't let on. She accepted the fact that America

33

was going to war and I was going to have to do my part. She might not have been happy about it but she was right by my side supporting me. We all had a job to do and the Army was going to be mine. So, our lives continued. After Billie, Renee was born May 4, 1946. Then Larry on February 9, 1952. She delivered all three of our children at Mercy Hospital, the same hospital where she was denied admission to nursing school. Interestingly, by the time each of our children were born the hospital bill was paid in advance, because when you found out you were pregnant, the hospital set you up on a budget payment plan and you paid so much per week toward the delivery and hospital bill.

When Renee was five months old we pulled into the long drive of what is now Clearview Golf Club on U.S. 30. We drove down the long lane and arrived at the old farmhouse that would become our home. Just as when I went to war, Marcella was right by my side. And by my side she stayed for 56 years. When we took our wedding vows I didn't realize the depth of blessings Marcella would bestow on my life. Till death us do part weren't just part of our vows, till death us do part meant facing together all of the trials, tribulations, triumphs, and joy of a steadfast relationship that lasted us a lifetime. It was only death that parted us.

Marcella dressed to the nines, circa '40s

Chapter Four: I'm In The Army Now

"What lies behind us and what lies before us are tiny matters compared to what lies within us." [4]

Emerson

Nothing could have prepared me for the experience of war. Likewise, nothing could have prepared me for the second-class treatment by Americans of an American citizen, who was literally laying his life on the line for his country, during WWII.

In a television interview in January 2000, famous Hollywood film director, Norman Jewison said, "The principle is wrong to ask someone to offer their life in the service of their country only for them not to be able to sit anywhere on the bus or buy a cup of coffee."

Right or wrong, that's the way it was.

The scales of justice, not in my favor, tipped early.

The Army had specific criteria for promotions to the rank higher than captain. No black man was promoted beyond the rank of captain because they didn't want a black man in a position to give a command to a white officer. Did they have criteria for who got weapons when? You bet. Black troops weren't issued weapons until the last minute, literally just before being shipped out. My conclusion was that a black man with a rifle was a little too scary for a lot of white officers and politicians.

I had high hopes to be assigned to one of the black units of the Army Air Corps training in Tuskeegee, Alabama. It would have been poetic returning to

Alabama to begin a new chapter in my life where it began. The Tuskeegee Airmen were an elite group and after basic training my brother Dempsey was stationed at Tuskeegee as a dental technician. He said they were a good unit, so of course it was my first choice when asked. When my name came up I was sent to another unit - - no appeals in the Army on assignments. Basically, I believe the Army let you think you had a choice and then they sent you exactly the opposite of where you wanted to go.

In those days the military was taking anyone they could get, not necessarily the cream of the crop. I was surprised at who they drafted. It was almost like they opened up the prison gates and drafted whatever walked out still breathing.

After our induction in Columbus, we traveled in segregated train cars to South Carolina. From Walterboro, South Carolina we were shipped off to Greenville and then returned to Walterboro for more training in the Quartermaster Corps. My brother Berry was a lieutenant with an ROTC commission in the 93rd Infantry and they did their basic training at Ft. Benning, Georgia.

During my second tour at Walterboro, South Carolina we were waiting to be shipped out and the base commander said we weren't ready to go to war; we hadn't even fired our rifles. So, to squeeze in our rifle practice to get ready for war we had to use the rifle range at night because the day schedule was filled.

After my second tour at Walterboro I was assigned to the base in Tallahassee, Florida. The train ride down to Florida was unsettling. I boarded the train with almost 100 other soldiers who had recently been released from the stockade, known in the military as the guardhouse. It was a fluke that I was on this train traveling to a new assignment and I wished I had been on another train. These guys were very tough.

The first altercation occurred as we backed into the station in Jacksonville. They started playing craps. The military police dropped in and ordered them to cease or their money would be seized. These guys dared the military police to try stopping them. The military police didn't exactly turn and run at the sight and threat of these soldiers, but they obviously considered the big picture and walked away. Smart boys.

I'd learned a little about cards and dice when I was a caddie, but there was no way I was going to jump in a game with these guys. I wasn't comfortable being around them. I wasn't afraid of them physically. I knew I could handle myself at 5'9" and 194 pounds, but there is wisdom in knowing what battles to fight and from which battles to walk away. There would be plenty of fighting and battles where we were going. No need to look for trouble when I knew it would find us.

Then a young lieutenant told us anyone who left the train would be court-martialed. What a joke. Seconds later there were only four of us left on the train, in spite of orders to stay on the train or be court-martialed. The rest of the motley crew had run off to town to drink and chase women, and whatever. They even had to hold the train from leaving until the military police could go to town and round up my fellow carousing, drunk soldiers. They simply didn't care and probably wished they were back in the guardhouse instead of heading to war.

Quickly I decided the best route for me was Officer Candidate School. As an officer you had more: more control, more money, and more respect. I was led to believe my chances were good. As it turned out, I had two chances, slim and none. I had an appointment to go before the review board at Ft. Jackson in Columbia, South Carolina on a Monday. The problem was I was ordered to report to my Port of Embarkation in New Jersey on Saturday. I was told not to worry about it. They said just resubmit your application. Well, my papers got lost. Not once, twice. Efficiency was definitely not the watchword of the Army at that time.

Shipping out was a heartbeat away. I had no idea what to expect. We were under orders not to contact anyone, but everyone did. It wasn't a matter of top-secret security; it was about their control. The Army wanted to keep you in line and they never seemed to pass up an opportunity to let you know who was in charge and who had control of your life.

I called Marcella and asked her to meet me before I left. She met me in New Brunswick, New Jersey at Camp Kilner. We went to New York and took in all the sights as if it were the honeymoon we could never afford to take. The city was huge and alive. It was also jammed with servicemen. People were friendly to a guy in uniform. We took the train to 42nd Street and went to the famous Stage Door Canteen. We tried to make the most of our time together but the war was looming over our heads and it was something that never left our minds. Saying goodbye to Marcella...well, I missed her even before I said goodbye. We were kept apart for 3 long years.

The Queen Mary was our transportation destination. Being land locked all my life I was amazed at the size, speed, and beauty of the vessel. Of course, getting to the ship was an uphill climb, literally. We had to march over a mile carrying our "A" bags, which weighed about 150 pounds. Then we had to climb up a long set of stairs equivalent to seven stories to board the ship. Thankfully there were no enemies on board to fight. We were too exhausted.

The Queen Mary, what a ride. During her construction in John Brown's shipyard on the River Clyde in Scotland, she was simply known as No. 534. Over 4,000 craftsmen worked on her and more than 10,000,000 rivets were driven home in the Queen Mary's construction. The Queen Mary is famous for 160,000 horsepower, service speed of 28.50 knots, 2,500 square feet of glass, over 2,000 portholes, and four 35-ton propellers. Each hand set turbine rotor contained 64,166 blades. The length of the Queen Mary was 1,019.5 feet, equaling over 300 yards, which equals 3 football fields. That's a big ship. I was going to sail across the Atlantic on this ship...the ship who Adolf Hitler had a standing offer of $250,000 to any U-boat crew that could sink her. [5]

Setting sail and gazing at the Statue of Liberty, I was filled with so many emotions. She was standing so stately in the harbor. I realized I was a part of history. I knew I was going to Europe for a war. Frankly, I had very little thought of ever coming back.

As a soldier I was going into the unknown. I

had no plans for the future. How could I plan for a future under those circumstances?

I also realized that my destiny was in the Lord's hands, not mine. I had no one to hold onto and it was a lonely, empty moment. By that time I was almost numb. My eyes were still fixed on the Statue of Liberty even though she was disappearing in the distance. I strained to keep her in my sights. The Statue of Liberty was the last visual connection I had with my homeland.

In awe I asked myself, "Will I ever see it again?"

Then I settled back into the reality of the situation. There were 23,000 troops on board with 16 men packed in staterooms designed for two people. Bunks ran three high up the side of each stateroom wall. It gave new meaning to the phrase "packed like sardines."

The September weather was perfect and the Queen Mary had a top speed of 35 knots. She was so fast that no escort ship could keep up with us, so we sailed along, zigzagging our way across the Atlantic. We changed course every seven minutes just in case a German U-boat would spot us.

Like on most ships, you try not to spend too much time in your cabin, especially when it was as crowded as ours. There was no segregation on board the ship; however since we all went over as units and there were only blacks in my unit, there were only blacks in my room. Approximately 120 men were in my trucking company. We were all in it together and managed to get along well.

The formal ballroom was converted into the dining hall and chow line. What a chow line! The line would open at 8:00 a.m. and run continuous throughout the whole day. Our rations were English and you had two choices, eat it or starve, actually, quite simple.

The Queen Mary was so big it was easy to get lost. You could walk for hours on the promenade deck and not know where you were. WW didn't just stand for world war; it also stood for wandering and waiting. The military police controlled the foot traffic and all you heard was "keep moving" because there was no strolling. We were all assigned life vests, "Mae Wests" as the guys called them. Many chose not to wear them until they would hear an unidentified plane flying overhead and our anti-aircraft guns opened up. Lucky for us we were the ones doing the shooting.

We came ashore at Greenoch, Scotland on the River Clyde near Glasgow three days later. I've always been keenly interested in history and geography, so it was thrilling to see this far away land that I had read so much about and wondered if I would ever see. So my European travels began.

From Greenoch, Scotland we went to Liverpool where I was stationed at Camp Maghull, Station 577, near the famous horserace track at Aintree Park, except there wasn't any racing going on during the war, just the war.

I came to respect the British. They are a tough people whom the Germans underestimated. When their cities were bombed they were clearing the rubble while they could still hear the engines of the Luftwaffe disappearing in the sky. It was amazing to see their determination. Our country has not faced a foreign invasion on our soil. We have two big oceans to protect us. Pearl Harbor was a tragedy for the United States but nothing compared to Hitler's Blitz.

It was at the Red Cross Service Club in Liverpool where I met Doc Kelker from Dover, Ohio, an All-American basketball player at Western Reserve. We became friends. The British were friendly too. They were also very hospitable to Americans, black or white.

In England they asked, "What can we do for you?"

Very different from back home where the greeting in the south was more like, "What are you doing here?"

The truth is, most Britons had never met a black American soldier face-to-face and that led to some very strange experiences. White American soldiers would tell people that we had tails and some, perhaps many, of the British believed them.

One day a young boy approached me and very politely wondered if he could ask me a question.

"Sergeant, do you have a tail?" he asked.

"No, but I bet you have a sister," I replied.

"Yes sir, I do" the boy said.

"And I bet she's dating a white American soldier, isn't she?"

"Yes, from the American Embassy," the boy said. "He told her that colored soldiers have tails."

I just shook my head; too sad to be mad.

This shameful bigotry was confirmed by a friend of mine, Lieutenant Fletcher, who told me a similar story. He was invited to a local home for dinner and when he arrived he was ushered into the parlor.

"Wait, wait," the lady of the house said as he entered the room. "Don't sit down yet. I'll get you a pillow."

"That's not necessary, this chair looks very comfortable," he said.

"Very well," the lady said. "I just didn't want you to hurt your tail."

Well, tails or no tails, things were starting to heat up as preparations were being made for the invasion of Normandy. Our unit, 1517th Quartermasters Mobile Aviation was transferred from Aintree Park to the Village of Cottingham, Station 585, near Hull, which was the largest port on the North Sea. A schoolmaster told me that this port was where Mary, Queen of Scots, once spent the night in a ditch in order to avoid capture and certain execution. I don't believe this knowledge impressed my friends.

I was a technical sergeant. That meant three stripes up and two down. I was an Operations Chief assigned to headquarters and my job was organizing and coordinating convoys and routing trucks all over England. We supplied the Army Air Corps and the Royal Air Force bases throughout England. Combat Wing Support would call in pick-up point orders and we delivered. Our trucks carried bombs, fuses, and other munitions. It was very dangerous work and when people got careless there were accidents. It was up to me to oversee the 11 different companies that we had control over during the invasion. When I would get a request for a convoy, I knew what was available from my daily roster and would coordinate all the trucks requested. Sometimes this meant negotiation with dispatchers. No matter how, the job had to get done. We worked around the clock.

My job included a lot of paperwork, like everything else in the service. It was stressful at times but I didn't face the dangers that some of the drivers, both black and white faced.

One day one of our trucks was carrying a load of 250-pound naval bombs. These were particularly dangerous because they were so sensitive and could detonate if dropped from a height less than four feet. The truck was a ragtop, which meant it had a canvas roof. It was headed down a hill when the brakes gave out, crashing into a bridge and the bombs tumbled out into a nearby field. It was nothing short of a miracle that none exploded. The driver was uninjured but it could have been a disaster. Suppose the accident had occurred in a town or village with women and children around?

One of my men was driving a truck loaded with bombs when he collided with a petrol truck. My man got out and ran back to warn the busload of people behind him. As he did, the truck exploded. It left a 25-foot crater in the middle of the road. One of the truck's axles was found a mile away; another miracle that no one was killed or injured.

From Cottingham our unit was moved across the Humber River to Briggs, Station 553. By now we had established a reputation as a unit that could get the dangerous jobs done under pressure. Our drivers were known as Rubber Booters. They put their foot on the gas pedal and kept it there. We transported Air Corps supplies for all the air bases and since so much of what we carried was considered vital we got special clearances from Headquarters.

A red ball sticker on the lead truck of the convoy identified our special clearances. When the military police would see the red ball sticker they waved us right through. Our unit started what became known as the Red Ball Express and after the war Hollywood made a movie about us. Naturally we were all thrilled and very proud. Naturally we never got a bit of the credit we were due. In the movie the Red Ball Express drivers were portrayed as white, not black. All of us Red Ball Express drivers were black.

The Red Ball Express was a good example of how, in some ways, the Army didn't see color. They'd give you jobs and responsibility that you couldn't get in civilian life. When a job needed to be done they didn't care what color you were. All they wanted to know was if you could get it done. A perfect example was a little guy we had in our unit by the name of Shepard from Mississippi. He couldn't read or write but he could work magic on a gearbox. I believe he was the best driver we had and he got plenty of tough assignments. The truth is, as good as he was, he wouldn't have been able to get a job washing trucks back in the U.S.A. The Army, however, didn't care about anything except whether Shepard could get a truck from point A to point B, and Shepard was a genius at that.

As the invasion approached, our unit was convoyed down to Ampfield Woods. It was a camouflage build up area near Southampton. Ampfield Woods was also a staging area near the English Channel. We went on detached service to SOS, Service of Supply, for the invasion of Normandy, France. None of us knew the exact date of the invasion but we all knew it was coming, and coming soon.

We were under strict orders not to discuss any

aspect of our work with anyone. The Nazis had spies everywhere. A lot of Germans had moved to the United States before the war and they had returned as spies. They acted and sounded like Americans. They could talk to you about your hometown or your favorite baseball team. For a guy facing death in a matter of days or weeks, having someone from back home to talk to, was not only tempting, but also comforting. The Nazis understood that and used it to their advantage.

Mail call was about the biggest thing you looked forward to every day, whether you were waiting to be called to the front lines or were in action. In today's world you can call home from anywhere in the world, but also send email as well. Back then a letter was your only contact with loved ones and receiving one really boosted your spirits. Marcella and my family were good about writing and sometimes they would include photos. You were always anxious to find out what was going on at home and my letters from home were the most precious things you can imagine. I treasured every one of them. I'd read them over and over, and all of the guys would share their letters with each other.

Two weeks before the invasion we began to bring troops down to the staging area. We ran those 1,100 trucks at full throttle twenty-four hours a day. Some of the trucks were carrying one-ton trailers behind them. During D-Day and the weeks that followed we were wearing out 125 to 200 trucks a week and that was just our unit.

Tension began to mount once we got the men to the Southampton staging area so we'd put them on the troop ships and then take them off a few hours later.

Waiting is tough on troops and putting them on and off the troop ships seemed to help take their minds off what was ahead of them and break up the tension and anxiety. It also helped keep the Nazis off balance for the spies who were watching.

They were never quite sure when or where we were going to attack. It was two o'clock in the morning on June 6, 1944 when our orders came down and we learned the invasion was on.

Once we started bringing the troops down all hell broke loose. Despite the best security and camouflage the Germans knew what was coming and began to pound us hard. The Germans were very methodical and when it came to bombings you could almost set your watch by them. Their planes would arrive around midnight every night. You'd hear them off in the distance as they approached the target, us. As the sound of their engines grew louder huge searchlights would come on and cut through the darkness. Then the anti-aircraft guns and the 105's would begin to erupt sending tracers slowly arching against the sky like fireworks. If it hadn't all been so deadly it would have been a beautiful sight to behold. When the bombs fell to earth it seemed like the pounding would never end. The ground would shake and even the trees would shake until you thought all the leaves would fall off. Your ears would ring and your body would ache from the pressure of the blasts. There would be a pause and just when you thought it was over another wave would fly over and it would start all over again. Earplugs were out of the question. If you had earplugs on you wouldn't have been able to hear a single order.

My closest call came two weeks before the invasion. The Germans knew something was going on and they stepped up the number of planes in their nightly bombing raids. We were bivouacked in tents, and a Canadian unit that we were not aware of, moved in below us. The Germans started a bombing run and the Canadian's opened up with their anti-aircraft guns. Between the German bombs, the Canadian's anti-aircraft, and our anti-aircraft guns the night sky was as light and bright as high noon.

What goes up must come down and a lot of the injuries we took in bombing raids were from shrapnel falling back to earth like rain showers. The only thing you could do to protect yourself in a bombing raid was to dig yourself a nice deep foxhole and scrunch down as low as possible. Foxholes could save your life, unless it was a direct hit.

In one raid a huge piece of shrapnel fell through the Colonel's tent that was right near ours. He wasn't hurt but one of the guys said we should go see if he was okay. Most guys decided to hell with the Colonel and dug deeper foxholes. I didn't get in the debate. I was too busy digging. Sometimes you aren't as brave as you think you are and common sense prevails.

Most of us were awake at 2:30 a.m. that morning because we watched the planes leaving and flying over us. The afternoon before, British Lancaster bombers were pulling gliders and carrying paratroopers who would be dropped inland behind the beaches. We knew if they were going, the main invasion force wouldn't be far behind. The waiting was over.

With the invasion underway we threw everything

we had into the effort. The trucks were running 24/7 bringing fresh troops and supplies from the staging areas to the docks. Not long after the first troops landed in France our trucks were still running 100% but our somber task and duty was bringing back our dead, wrapped in mattress covers, to the large refrigerated tents where they were stored.

No one got used to the sheer number of dead and wounded. You wouldn't be human if you did. You become numb. It's like being bombed night after night. After awhile you become desensitized to the whole situation. You still feel the fear and uncertainty but you unconsciously block out the atrocities of war and pray you escape it. If you survive, you don't get over the numbness overnight. I was still numb for a long time after the war. I remember Marcella telling me that someone had died. I would just think, so what?

I had prepared myself to die and sympathy was slow coming back to me. People who have never seen combat or been in a war cannot possibly begin to understand how awful and devastating it is.

I was ordered up to an air base hospital in East Anglia from Tostock, Station 502, for a routine physical and arrived a few hours after a squadron of our bombers had returned from Germany. The orderly told me they had been badly shot up. Men were crying out for morphine, literally screaming and begging for anything to help ease the pain. Orderlies said they had orders to check dog tags and verify identification before they gave them morphine. Soon they were removing their dog tags. The floors had been a pool of blood but by the time I got there they had been scrubbed down and there was nothing left to witness the horror of the event. Even now, more than 50 years later, I still think about that hospital and those boys.

I'm not a pacifist. Hitler and his allies needed to be beaten, but when I watch people who have never seen the horrors of war say we should send kids off to die it makes me sick to my stomach. When we were over in Vietnam I never had a gripe with the guys who wouldn't go. I'd pat them on the back. That war was a disgrace. The boys that were killed and wounded over there deserve our honor, love, and support - - but not the people who sent them. They deserve our scorn.

One day I got my first close-up look at the enemy; SS troopers that had been captured and shipped to England. They passed through Southampton on a train. We had heard about the SS and what they did but the sight of them was still a shock and made me angry. They weren't soldiers. There's honor in being a soldier. They looked like animals and from what I've read maybe they were.

Like most folks who fought in the war I've been asked if I have any hard feelings toward the Germans. I suppose the answer is, like any other group of people, there are good ones and bad ones and you have to try to keep that in perspective. My animosity was toward the Nazis. There is no pardoning what they did and when you hear people in this country, especially kids, say they are Nazis and want to be part of the Neo-Nazis, well you know they must be ignorant.

After D-Day General Patton and his boys broke out and swept south of Paris keeping us busy trying to keep him supplied. The fact is Patton might have marched right on into Berlin if they had let him have the fuel and his own way.

Eventually we were moved up to East Anglia as the bombing of Germany intensified. The bombings lasted around the clock with the Americans hitting the Nazis during the day and the Brits bombing them at night. Some of the targets were the submarine pens on the Denmark coast. We hit those with concrete piercing bombs that were so big it took two trucks to haul just one bomb. When I saw those bombs and saw the British Lancaster bombers, which were the only plane big enough to carry them, taking off at all hours I didn't need to read the newspapers to know Hitler's days were numbered.

Sure enough on April 30, 1945 Hitler committed suicide and Germany surrendered a week later. The war in Europe was over. We were all ecstatic but we didn't have much time to celebrate. We were going back to the States for a short leave and then heading to the Far East to fight the Japanese.

Anytime we were stationed in one place long enough for me to get a little down time I would try to find a golf course. In Great Britain it seemed like every small place had at least a nine-hole course, and while most of them were private, they were always good about letting us play. Most of the time they would just let us go out, but some places like Inverness, Scotland required we play with members, which was fine with me. Even though I was playing with clubs borrowed from the Red Cross and was out of practice I still managed to play pretty well. In fact, the British were quite surprised to see that a black man could play as well as I did.

One day I went over to the Southampton Golf Club near our base in Basset. I was really on my game and when I came to the tenth hole, a downhill par-three near the clubhouse, I almost made a hole-in-one. As I walked to the eleventh tee all of a sudden there was a gallery. By the time I hit my drive there were forty people watching. I hit a beauty, long and straight. They even followed me for a few holes.

The British have a very proper approach to the game that I really loved. I was playing at Bury St. Edmond's one afternoon when I hit my ball off into the tall grass. As I was searching for the ball I noticed a foursome of women coming up the fairway behind me and I motioned for them to hit up. When they reached me one politely told me they were playing through.

"We're playing in a competition," one explained.

When I told them by all means, please play through, they thanked me very nicely and went on their way.

As I mentioned before the British were very polite. They were also quite curious when it came to black soldiers. One day a couple invited me to join them for lunch after a round of golf at their club, Bassett Golf Club. During the course of conversation the woman asked me how I was being treated in England.

"You shouldn't be bothered if the people around here ignore you," she said. "People in the south of England aren't at all friendly. We moved here from London 10 years ago and I still don't know my neighbors."

She was Cockney, who is someone who lives within the sound of Big Ben in London, and her husband was from Hampshire. He was the only reason she was in the south of England.

Sometimes I was asked if I planned to try to play professional golf when I got back home. In the beginning I'd try to explain what it was like in the States but after awhile I just gave up. It was too complicated to explain what racism was like in the United States, and besides, I was out there to have some fun and relax.

I played a lot of nice courses around England: Ipswich, Southampton, Cambridge, Bury St. Edmond's and a few others. They all had their own unique character. I played Inverness in Scotland because I was interested in the history of the course, but just being out there on any course was idyllic. That, plus the kind and humane way I was treated re-ignited my love for the game. In Great Britain I was seen as a golfer who happened to be black. Back home I was a black man trying to play a white man's game.

We sailed back to America on the Alexander Graham Bell, a liberty ship. She was no Queen Mary but I didn't mind. I didn't have to worry about German submarines or air attacks this time across the Atlantic. It was a nice leisurely trip and all the guys were in good spirits.

Halfway across we were relaxing on deck and talking about our experiences in England and one of the guys brought up a time when I had canceled his leave because I needed him to drive an important convoy.

He said, "I should throw you overboard."

Next thing I knew two other guys joined in and they carried me to the side of the ship and said they were going to toss me over. They actually hung me out over the water. I wasn't worried. I knew they were only kidding because I really tried to take care of my men and they appreciated that. Whenever I could, I'd cut my men some slack by deadlining their vehicles, which meant time off because when you were assigned to a vehicle no one else drove it. So if the truck was deadlined for a few days the driver had time off. They repaid me by going all out when I needed them. That sense of teamwork was one of the good things I remember from the war.

I don't know if any of us really believed our service in the war would make life different for us back in the States, but if we did, our illusions were quickly shattered. We came into the port of Boston to Camp Miles Standish where there were a lot of German POW's. We boarded a train for Camp Attelbury in Indiana. After 30 days recuperation-leave back home, we went back to Indiana and then were shipped to Brookley Field in Mobile, Alabama. When the train crossed the border from Indiana into Kentucky we got our warm welcome back to America, a segregated train station in Louisville and seats only for blacks in a Jim Crow car for the rest of the trip. This particular train car was the first car in back of the steam engine. It was not priority seating.

When we got to Louisville we blacks were sent to the left side of the waiting room and whites were sent to the right. A sick feeling came over me. After all we'd been through, after all we'd seen, and after all we'd done for our country it was worse than a slap in the face. Years later, my children asked why we didn't protest. Well, we were from a different time period. We were conditioned to respect the law, even if the law didn't respect us. I believe that black soldiers were the most loyal group of Americans because we wanted so much to believe in America.

When we got to Mobile, the uniform we wore and everything we had done in England didn't amount to anything. One very hot and humid day a black field ordinance officer went into the headquarters and saw a refrigerated water fountain marked "Whites Only." Next to it was an old marked up "Colored" one. He began to drink from the refrigerated fountain and was stopped by a military police man and was told it was against the rules.

"Why?", he asked. "It's government property isn't it?"

Yes it was, and it didn't matter.

He went into the base commander's office over the incident and the commander told him, "I'm sorry lieutenant, you are in the south."

The lieutenant went right back out and got himself another drink at the refrigerated water fountain. He was wearing the same .45 that the military police man was carrying.

There were other things that still bother me to this day. In Mobile, when we were given our lightweight uniform, Summer Tans, we got salvaged clothes that had been patched and worn before. The German POW's also got Summer Tans but their uniforms were brand new.

Then there was the movie theater. The POW's could go anytime they pleased, and did so often with one of the WAC's, a member of the Women's Army Corp. The POW's dated our WAC's. Our hours for the movie theater were restricted.

As a friend of mine said, "It was too bad we had to go to Europe to fight one enemy just to come home and face another; racism."

In August, we dropped the atomic bombs on Hiroshima and Nagasaki. The Japanese surrendered. I was ecstatic. People who say Harry Truman shouldn't have dropped those bombs are nuts. They weren't the ones who had their lives on the line, and they weren't the ones going to be chopped up. The way I see it, the only mistake old Harry made was not dropping the bombs sooner.

When VJ Day came my orders were changed and I was sent to Patterson Field in Dayton, Ohio. I must have done a pretty good job for the Army because they tried to get me to re-enlist.

"What do you have against me?" I laughingly asked the officer.

I'm proud I did my duty but I was ready to go home to Marcella and Billy. It was time to get on with my life now that I was finally back in the USA.

For love of family...

and country

Chapter Five: Back In The USA

"I think the angels care for us best
when we decide to do something new
or unexpected that could make a dream come true." [6]

D. Combs

I was back in the USA. After my discharge from the Army I was ready to get on with my life and golf was going to be a part of it. I loved the game. I had it bad for golf and I knew it from the time I was nine and started my golfing career as a caddy with my brother Berry, to playing every day all summer long with Doc Casey, to captain of the golf team at Minerva High School, and right to the golf team and sports history at Wilberforce University.

My experience playing the historic and beautiful courses in England and Scotland re-ignited my desire to simply play. The warm and hospitable way I was welcomed and treated in Europe made me think that maybe, just maybe, it might be possible for me to do what I loved most when I returned to the States, play golf - - no matter what.

Marcella, Billy and I were living on Dudley Avenue where Marcella and Billy lived while I was overseas. After I settled back in from the Army I decided to give my dream a try.

In the entire area there were only two courses I could play and feel welcome, Edgewater in Minerva and The Elms in Massillon. What bothered me was that I had played on all the courses in the area as a caddy and in high school for our golf team matches.

After my return from the war and back in the U.S.A., I was never actually turned down, but you knew you were not welcome and not wanted. I simply was not encouraged to play golf anywhere else other than Edgewater or The Elms.

Probably one of the defining moments of me deciding to just build my own golf course occurred during a humiliating experience at Tam O'Shanter, a well-known golf course in northeastern Ohio.

Harry Moots was the pro at the time. When I showed up to play I put him on the spot because they had a policy not to let people of color play the course. I was well known in the area however, and it made it difficult for him to turn me down. He didn't turn me down, but he didn't go out of his way to make me feel that welcome. Neither did the other players on the course.

A classic example was when I came upon a foursome and asked if I could play through. The two men in the foursome were cordial but the two women turned their backs on me. Tam O'Shanter not only had a policy not to let people of color play, they also had a card system. They distributed membership cards only to whites. The ownership passed on their attitude through their exclusive policy.

This is the same course that turned Joe Louis away when he was heavy weight champion of the world. Think about what a degrading and humiliating experience that was for Joe Louis.

Later I talked to a friend of mine, Bud Labus, from Minerva and told him about my experience.

His comment was, "Harry Moots just plain didn't want you there."

Well, I had too much self-respect for that. It was obvious if I wanted to play golf I would have to build my own course. You know, I never thought how incredulous that might sound. Build your own course. With what? I didn't quite know how, or where, or when. What I did know was that I resolved that no one would keep me from playing the game I loved. No one. I didn't care how long it took or what I had to do to build the dream. All I knew was that I was going to build my own golf course somehow, someway. No one was going to control me or tell me what I could or could not do.

When I first returned to Timken after the war I had no idea I would stay for 23 years, mostly the 3-11 shift. I worked at the well at the corner of Navarre and Deuber Avenues. They had five, sixteen-feet horizontal pumps mounted inside the 16-inch well that ran seven days a week, 24 hours a day. The well had a pit and a bulldozer with a 14-foot blade that Dallas Mount used to dig the pit. The bulldozer dug out the sand and gravel. They used a Marine diver from Detroit to unclog and clean the feeder pipes that came from the bottom of the well.

While I was working at the well there was talk of a layoff. The conversations about the layoff were intentionally discussed in front of me.

"The black fellow would be laid off first," the gossipers said.

Concerned about my status, I went to Mr. Greene to discuss the matter. He pulled out his employee roster and assured me that 15 or 20 others would have to go first before it came down to me. In fact, according to Mr. Greene's roster the big talkers would have been laid off before me.

With determination Marcella and I began to look for a piece of land that would be suitable to live on and build a golf course. Whether it was coincidence, luck or the will of God, and I prefer to believe the latter, it is often amazing how happenings occur.

On Sundays we would drive back and forth from Canton to my parents in Minerva on U.S. 30. We always passed by a certain piece of property on the way and I would always turn to Marcella and remark that this beautiful farmland would certainly be a perfect setting for a golf course. I couldn't get over the terrain, but we figured the owners would never sell it.

Then one day as we were looking through the newspaper trying to find suitable acreage we read about a farm that was for sale just near East Canton. As we drove out trying to find the farm that was for sale we passed by the dairy farm we had so long admired. Back home we went and with a quick call to the real estate agent we discovered the two properties were one in the same. Miracles, that's what I was thinking.

We drove out to have a better look at the 78 acres that had been a Whipple Farm. Tom Elliott, the farmer who owned it at that time was leaving and going back to Warsaw, Virginia, his wife's home.

Mr. Elliott was trying to tell me about the house but my main interest of course was the outside property for a golf course. I really had very little interest in the house. I left Marcella in the farmhouse and I set out to do a walk-through of the property. I walked over to what is now hole 6, which was old 4. It was right in the middle of a soybean field and I could see the entire property from there. I went back in to talk to Marcella.

The buildings on the property were badly rundown but my interest was in the land and it was perfect to me. Before I left that day I had the nine-hole course already designed in my mind's eye. We knew we had found the property that would become the focus of all of our lives.

Getting a loan for the property was a different story. Once again the scales tipped, and not in my favor. My friends from Minerva had told me they had received GI loans. I was a GI. I served my country. I went to war for it. So I went looking for one myself. Bank after bank told me there was no such thing. Can you imagine?

I was disheartened perhaps, but not devastated. I certainly was not willing to give up. There had to be a way to buy that property. I just had to figure out how. I finally convinced two black doctors to go in with me as equal partners. My partners were Dr. Ross from Canton who delivered all three of our children and Dr. Malloy from Massillon, right next door to Canton. I had been teaching them how to play golf at Edgewater and got them hooked on the game and they were very interested in the idea of having a golf course. The only hitch was I didn't have the capital. Then my brother Berry took out a loan on his house to give me my third of the investment for the deal. The papers were signed in September 1946. I was one step closer to making my dream come true.

First we would move in and then the work would begin. I knew what I was getting into and I rose to meet the challenge. I was not apprehensive of the task that lay before me. It was an enormous endeavor that scares me to think of today at age 83. To embark on something like that with nothing. What was I thinking? It was not only an enormous endeavor for me, but for Marcella, Billy, Renee, and Larry. Every one of them would pick up the beat to my drum. And the drumbeat was hard and fast for years. That meant untold sacrifices for my dream.

We moved to the farm on October 1, 1946. It was a cold, crisp morning. We drove down the lane and stepped out of the car. We looked around and took stock of our new home. There was the century-old farmhouse with a large bank barn in the back needing every repair imaginable. There was also a milking barn in the front and a chicken coop between the two barns in total disrepair. We had a large silo and the real bonus was the springhouse with water so sweet that people would travel from miles around to fill their jugs. The storage building would become our workshop.

When we first moved to Clearview you couldn't see the highway from the house. You had to go upstairs and look out a bedroom window in order to see the highway. A big sweet-potato patch grew where the golf cars are now positioned. Trees and tree stumps lined the eastside of the lane. There was an abundance of fruit trees: apple trees, a Georgia peach, yellow and red plum, a great big Northern Spy apple tree, and cherry trees. There were also Concord grape arbors. North of the house were pear trees and right in the front yard towered an Early Transparent apple tree. Gardens graced the land north and south of the house. Up the hill and to the east was an orchard filled with peach trees and an apple grove, the north side of the house was dense with locust trees.

The chicken coop was overflowing with white

rock chickens running all over the place. There had been a farm auction after the property sale and they had sold everything except for the fast-on-their-feet chickens that were hiding in the tall grass where no one could catch them, so they stayed. I figured we might get tired of eating chicken but we would not starve.

As we entered the south kitchen door of the farmhouse there was a combination coal and electric range that the previous owners soon removed. The kitchen also had a big cast iron sink with a pitcher-pump at the end facing the east window. The house consisted of four bedrooms, a dining room, living room, parlor, and kitchen. A brick chimney was in each room. The heat from the coal furnace moved upward from the basement through floor registers. The pipes from the furnace were bad and needed to be replaced immediately. That first night at the farmhouse we all slept together in one bed to stay warm.

There was no time to waste. Everything had to be put into motion right away. Project number one had emerged; putting in a new furnace that was the first thing I did. Project number two was the plumbing. There was water in the kitchen from a pitcher pump but no bathroom. We used the outhouse for over a month until I could put a pump in the reservoir in the basement to get pressure for indoor plumbing. I had to measure the pipe, get it threaded, and do all the calculations. I also had to install a septic system.

Once the family had heat and indoor plumbing I could get to work on the golf course. At the same time I was doing repairs to the farmhouse, I made arrangements to have the land tilled right away in order for it to be ready for spring. Another step closer to making my dream come true.

I had walked the property as a prospective buyer. I knew how I wanted to design the course. Now I had to put it on paper. I had to secure maps from the county but there weren't any topographical maps in 1946.

I sat down and drew the first nine holes. I worked everything from scale. Using overlay graph paper I used each square on the graph paper for a yard. The original layout of the ground was on our first scorecards.

I would take advantage of the terrain and natural hazards. The greens would have to be designed from the limestone outcropping to take advantage of the natural underground spring, since there would be no irrigation system. I wanted to avoid having holes that paralleled one another. That's too dangerous because most golfers aren't exactly what you might call straight hitters. Besides making the holes interesting and challenging, I also wanted to spare as many trees as possible. My idea was to make the course fair for the average player but challenging for the better golfer.

People often say Clearview is a very natural looking golf course and I consider that a compliment. Part of the reason that's true is that it was such an ideal piece of land to begin with, but the truth is we didn't have the time, money, or equipment to move a lot of dirt all over the place. The result is holes that just look like they are supposed to be there. They fit your eye, not fight it, like so many of the courses do today.

I had lined up two farmers that I paid to help with the plowing. They were also neighbors. John

Nieman had a John Deere and Bill Zwick was an Allis Chalmers man. Smitty from ACME Sand & Gravel ran the bulldozer and pulled the tree stumps out of the ground that lined the lane.

I was definitely doing something new and unexpected. I was ready to break ground and one step closer to making my dream come true. I could feel the angels start to gather. The fluttering of their wings was oh so comforting. Lord knows I would need their help.

Eyes on the prize

balancing life at Timken

Chapter Six: Groundbreaker

There are hermit souls that live withdrawn
In the place of their self-content;
There are souls like stars, that dwell apart,
In a fellowless firmament;
There are pioneer souls that blaze the paths
Where the highways never ran-
But let me live by the side of the road
And be a friend to man.
Excerpt from the "House by the Side of the Road"
Samual Walter Foss
public domain, 1899

In many ways my passion made me a pioneer soul of sorts. I continued to work at Timken every day from 3-11, come home and rest and rise at dawn. I could hardly wait for daybreak each morning. At early light I would be out working the course and work until I had to leave for Timken. There was little time for anything else.

At one point, we figured out that between Timken and the golf course I was working 18 hours a day, seven days a week. Sometimes I think my dream consumed me. Some days, I didn't even know if I had eaten.

All that time and hard work never bothered me. Not with Marcella right by my side and the children growing up. Clearview was definitely a family project and it seems that I've spent my whole life striving to climb to a better life, refusing to accept the standard of the time. I wanted to make a difference and I felt deep down inside that Clearview would do that.

In the spring of 1947, when the ground was still

soft, I pulled out all of the old farm fence posts with my bare hands, one by one. Picking up every stone by hand was par for the course. Slowly the ground I broke was becoming a golf course.

I seeded every fairway and fertilized them with my own hand-mixed fertilizer. I knew the type of grass I wanted and I knew the germination time. Initially, I planted Red-Chewing fescue and Highland bent grass. At first, all we had were hand mowers to cut and groom Clearview - - what a job!

The original greens were all Seaside bent grass. In fact, over the years we have seeded with Highland bent, Astoria bent, and Seaside bent. At one time we integrated and over seeded the fairways with Highland bent. The greens over the last 50 years have been Seaside bent, Pencross, and now Lofts-93, developed at Rutgers University. Lofts-93 exhibits the strongest resistance to extreme temperatures. Two small greens, holes 7 and 8 are currently planted with A-6 bent grass.

We officially opened for play in mid-April of 1948. While I was pleased with how far we had come I was also frustrated at the same time, because I wanted to build a second nine and make some major improvements. I wanted to make the course profitable and Dr. Ross and Dr. Malloy were more interested in a place of leisure and recreation. They did not understand the business concept. Even though we were equal partners they forced me to pay for any changes or improvements out of my own pocket that I really couldn't afford. Finally, 10 years after our original partnership had been formed I bought them out and then added another 52 acres for the second nine holes.

In addition to my family, I was blessed with good friends all my life that stood by me. They worked right by my side. Euley Glenn is one of those incredible people. He's been a part of Clearview since the beginning.

Euley was born December 29, 1921 in Dothan, Alabama. He attended Daniel Payne College for two years in Birmingham, which was part of the AME Church. He fell in love with a girl from Selma, Alabama who had family in Canton. Her name was Katie and she had the sweetest voice you ever heard. They were married May 14, 1944. Euley and Katie had two children, Sharon and Harold.

It is important that you understand the era Euley is from so that you know how similar our experiences were with society. We respected all levels of society and working class, but no one let us forget we were black.

Euley is an all around sportsman. While still living in Dothan, Alabama he played semi-pro baseball all over the south during the summer for the Boston Braves farm team. Preston Johnson, now 90 years old, owned the Braves farm team and paid Euley $50 a week to play ball during the summers of 1940-1942 before he went on to college.

In 1958 he bought his first set of golf clubs from me and he still uses them to this day. They are a Billy Burke set. Euley also had a full-time job at Hoover where he worked for 40 years. During the decades that he helped me, he worked the 11:00 p.m.- 7:00 a.m. shift. He would get off work, go home, have a quick bite of breakfast that Katie would have waiting for him and he would be at Clearview by 8:15 a.m. He would work all day by my side until 3:00 p.m. Euley would then go home, get some sleep and be back at work at Hoover by 11:00 p.m.

He worked like that seven days a week year in and year out, except for one day of the year, the first day of hunting season. You see, one year Euley was out working on old hole 3, now 5 the first day of hunting season and some hunter's shotgun pellets zinged past him pretty darn close. He figured, just to be on the safe side, that that would be one day each year not to expect him to pull in the lane.

Euley mowed all the greens. We started out with a Toro greens mower. We still have that original mower but it is now retired. He also mowed greens with our Jacobsen mower. In later years he was always a volunteer to help with golf outings and tournaments. Whatever was going on at Clearview, Euley was there to help. Clearview was just as important to him as his job was at Hoover.

I told you I felt the angels gathering, well they did. And one of the very best things they did was send Euley to me. I met him in 1946 and we've been friends ever since.

Euley's life has been built on his family, his job, and Clearview. Our camaraderie defies description. It was there, year in and year out, decade after decade. Why you might ask? What was in it for him?

When asked Euley said, "Being with Mr. Powell and knowing what he had been through to try and build a golf course you could not do anything else except respect the man for seeing into the future. Obviously he must have sensed what Clearview would mean to our history and the legacy it would create. Bill stood firm for what he believed in. He believed in his dream. In spite of being ostracized by everyone in Canton, black and white. Why, folks even used to refer to Clearview as the nigger nine. Can you imagine the stupidity in that cruelty? I defended him all the time. That was fine by me because Bill stood by his rules: play by my rules or play someplace else. That's probably why he is still here today. Clearview is and always has been an open course and anyone who wanted to play could. But make no mistake, Bill had rules and regulations."

Euley's trusted friendship all these years has helped me stay the course. I laugh when he tells his version of what Clearview would be today if I had given up or given in or worse yet listened to the public.

"Bill Powell would have had a world-class garden instead of a historic and legendary American golf course. What he has accomplished has been to make an impossible dream come true," says Euley.

Euley's faith is a big part of what makes him the kind of man he is. Now he's not a religious fanatic but he does believe that there is a God somewhere, someplace and that same God has been with him and me fighting the odds. When asked what philosophy he lives his life by he will tell you it's a philosophy he learned as a freshman at Daniel Payne College from Dean Calhoun.

He said, "Euly, there is something about you I like and I want you to read and learn this poem."

The line from the poem "House by the Side of the Road," that captures Euly's philosopy reads, "Let me live by the side of the road and be a friend to man." [7]

Well, he's done that all right, for many others

and me. His philosophy comes from a poem titled "House by the Side of the Road" by Samual Walter Foss in 1899. This poem could really be used as a yardstick for life. To measure what we do, what we can do, and how we do it. It's not enough to do anything we can for our fellow man we must do everything. Euley proved that.

I met my other lifetime friend Ralph Petros in 1935. I was a senior at Minerva High School when Ralph transferred in from Akron North. He was a state-wrestling champion at Akron North and when he transferred to Minerva High School we were on the golf team together. We became friends from the instant we met. From that day in 1935 we became lifelong friends until Ralph passed from this life to the next in 1986. For 51 years we were the best of friends in every situation that life presented. Everybody that knew Ralph knew I was his best friend and people knew not to ever say anything questionable or derogatory about me. He made it a point to let people know who his best friend was. One of Ralph's brothers even said to Ralph that he was closer to me than he was to his own brother.

Ralph never played golf anywhere but Clearview, except for a concrete tournament he played in once a year. He even left his clubs here and when the concrete tournament would roll around each year he would call up and say he was coming by to get his clubs for the tournament and as soon as the tournament was over he would bring them back on his way home.

Ralph and I were such good friends it was coincidental that we were the exact same size and height. We even wore the same odd size shoe, 7 1/2 EEE. He was the kind of friend who would give you the shirt off his back, and often did. Anytime I would compliment him on a nice pair of shoes, or whatever, he would give it to me on the spot. One time he left here bare foot because he took the shoes that I admired right off his feet. I finally had to stop saying anything about what he had on.

On one occasion Renee needed to get to a National United Golf Association tournament in Boston. I was driving her but I didn't think my car at the time was road worthy enough for that kind of trip. I was already in the market for a good used car but just hadn't found one yet.

I mentioned it to Ralph and he said, "Here, take the keys to my car and go."

Ralph had just gotten a new Cadillac and I don't think he had ever taken it out of town himself. I told him we might be gone for over a week.

He said, "I don't care if you're gone two or three weeks, take it."

He had it washed and polished, filled it up with gas and had it ready for me the next day with insurance papers in the glove box. That was the kind of friend Ralph was. He was like a twin brother to me. We shared such a special closeness. I'm sure we were soul friends. He was such a good hearted and generous spirit.

Ralph was at Clearview every week and we golfed together. It's a good thing too, for that may have helped keep me sane. I was working all of the time and when Ralph came out he would insist I take a break and play golf with him. I thank him to this day for that. We were so close we even knew each other's thoughts. There's not a day that goes by that I don't think of him and miss him. What a friend.

Ralph loved golf and often played with the guys from Cadiz. They have been dear friends for over 50 years and were part of the original players at Clearview. Cadiz is about 50 miles from here and is the home of Clark Gable. In fact, Clark Gable's house is still there. The group from Cadiz has been playing here every weekend, sometimes twice, with two or three foursomes. They had so many golfers we had to have a Cadiz Day each season.

It all started when Howard Broadus, who I played golf with on my college team at Wilberforce, came to Clearview. They all came to Clearview over the years, but Howard was the first. He told Bill Mason and Doc Tyler about the course and they decided to check it out. The original Cadiz group members were: Bill Mason, Vinny Wheeler, and Roscoe Wyatt. Others that joined the group and who have played here faithfully for decades include: Charles Brooks, Sam Taylor, Rim Mallory and Larry Jones, who headed up the four Jones' boys. Over the years we have all had great fun and now have great golfing memories.

In the beginning I'd say that about 99 percent of the golfers at Clearview were white. I always figured that if I built a good enough golf course people wouldn't care what color the man was who designed or built it. It's funny, but I don't think it ever occurred to me that white folks would not support Clearview in any way.

There have been a few problems over the years. Sometimes people might yell racial slurs as they drove past the course or we would have vandals who stole flagsticks from the greens from time to time, but I think that happens at a lot of courses. Mostly, people have been very supportive.

I remember the time my friend Henry Hein from Orchard Hills, a private club in Canton, came out to play. He said he'd heard good things about the course and wanted to give it a try. After he had been out there quite a while I began to get worried about him. I was afraid he might have had a heart attack so I drove out looking for him. I found him out on the course weeding dandelions off the 4th green. That's the kind of people I've been surrounded by.

It was hard work, for all of us. Many times my family suffered because of the hardship and expense of trying to design, build, and operate a golf course. We had to endure.

Everyone contributed what he or she could right from the very beginning. By the time the kids were eight they were all driving tractors and working on the course. Marcella was the clubhouse and office manager and managed all our affairs. I ran the course, taught golf everyday, and ran junior tournaments for kids of all ages for over 25 years. Billie worked continually on the course and never stopped until he left for California in 1966.

Renee joined the LPGA in 1967 and is now an LPGA/PGA professional, as well as head pro at Clearview. My son Larry has been the course superintendent since 1971, in addition to holding down a full-time job with the U.S. postal service. This course encircled us all.

I had taken a risk and gone out on a limb for my dream and my family was wrapped up in the dream very tight. I sure wasn't going to quit. Being a groundbreaker did not come without its price.

The golfing Powell family (1960)) L-R: Billy, Marcella, Larry, Mr. P and Renee

Chapter Seven: 81° Longitude, 40° Latitude

"America's Course…a course
where the only color that matters
is the color of the greens."

William J. Powell

To be precise, the exact location of Clearview is 81°, 15 minutes, 00 seconds longitude and 40°, 46 minutes, 30 seconds latitude. This is where you will find America's Course. A course where all are welcome, a course where the only color that matters is the color of the greens.

I built Clearview as a public course to provide anyone who wanted to play golf the opportunity to do so and feel welcome. It's an opportunity that was denied me and resulted in my determination to just build my own course and put the fair back in fairway.

Once you pull in the drive you travel down a long straight lane that brings you in front of the clubhouse. You wind around through a majestic greeting of whispering pines and find yourself in the parking lot. There are two entrances to the clubhouse. One is on the north side of the building where the golf carts rest when not on the course. Another entrance is on the west side and is graced by flowerbeds of annuals and perennials that smile as you walk by. You know you've found a home once you're there. This was especially true when Marcella was here. She made anyone who walked through the door feel at home and hundreds of people referred to her as Mom. She is deeply missed by every golfer who ever knew her.

Once you've paid your greens fees and rented a

pull cart for your clubs or a golf car, you head out the west entrance to the first tee where our American flag marks America's course. This course represents a thought that people are people, all of us. There is no race card to play here, just a scorecard.

I originally designed the course for nine holes in 1946 on 78 acres. In 1978 I redesigned it for eighteen. Building and maintaining this course in harmony with the land and the environment has always been a priority and a tradition well established at Clearview. The lay of the land and its resources have always been its foundation and one reason for its beauty (See Appendix for environmental survey).

Now, for all you serious golfers out there, let's get technical. Here are the course statistics:

Par: 69; 5,890 yards

Rating: 67.2

Slope: 105

Soil Conditions: Clay

Greens: Lofts 93 and A-6 bent grass

Green cut/speed: 090

Stimpmeter reading: Close to 12 with surfaces as low as 90/1000 of an inch

Greens constructions: Push-up

Tees: Ryegrass; cut to .350 inch

Fairways: Bent grass, poa, and ryegrass; 40 yards average width; cut to .550

Rough: Bluegrass, rye, and fescue

Bunkers: None

Water Hazards: 2 streams

Irrigation: None

Water source: Ponds

Turf vehicles: Club Car
Architect: William J. Powell (1946)
Superintendent: Larry Powell
Professional: Renee Powell

Okay, now we're ready to go on a tour of historical Clearview. After 50 years, it's still a challenging course and a thrill for me to play. I invite you to call us for a tee time. We look forward to meeting you.

Hole 1
Yards: 360
Handicap: 9
Par: 4

Description: This was a par 3 and is now par 4. It's a nice easy par 4 with a lateral stream running three-quarters the length of the hole. The green can be a hard green to putt depending on the placement of the pin. Since the course is not long we try to make the course more challenging, especially with undulating greens for each hole.

All the greens have breaks in them. There is a Crimson maple planted at this hole and Hole 18, the beginning and end, in honor and memory of Marcella. Hugh Chronister planted them. He brought the trees out, asked where we wanted them, dug the holes, and planted them.

Hole 2
Yards: 128
Handicap: 17
Par: 3

Description: This hole has the largest green on the course and pin placement can be at a premium. It is not an easy birdie hole.

Hole 3
Yards: 405
Handicap: 4
Par: 4

Description: Hole 3 is a sloping fairway from right to left. It is a good par 4 and a good golf hole. A stream crosses right in front of the green. The green can be challenging but if the pin is placed to the front edge of the green it is more difficult.

Hole 4
Yards: 439
Handicap: 6
Par: 4

Description: Hole 4 is a very good par 4. This hole was old 2. You play to a rollaway green and you must throw the ball up on the green in order to hold it.

Hole 5
Yards: 145
Handicap: 16
Par: 3

Description: Hole 5 is a short par 3. This hole was old 3. The green really is sloped and if you are playing to a prevailing wind it is an easy 3 putt. It is one of the trickiest putting greens on the course. It is also one of the smallest.

Hole 6
Yards: 326
Handicap: 13
Par: 4
Description: This hole is a relatively easy par 4 but deceiving. It was old 4. You have out of bounds on the right and you must throw the ball on the green. A grassy knoll surrounds the back of the green.

Hole 7
Yards: 365
Handicap: 8
Par: 4
Description: This is a straightaway hole, formerly 5, crossing the creek with out of bounds to the right. It can be a challenging hole and is the flattest putting green on the entire course.

Hole 8
Yards: 268
Handicap: 15
Par: 4
Description: This is a very short par 4 and old 6. This hole can be driven but pin placement can be made very difficult. You never want to get above the hole.

Hole 9
Yards: 394
Handicap: 2
Par: 4
Description: This was formerly 7. It is a straightaway hole, with a drive down into the flat; it is

a short iron to the green. Watch out for the large oak at the corner of the creek.

Hole 10
Yards: 426
Handicap: 5
Par: 4

Description: This is a nice 4 and old 8. This hole can play tough with prevailing winds. It has a large green that is easy to putt.

Hole 11
Yards: 409
Handicap: 7
Par: 4

Description: Hole 11 is a par 4. It was old 9. This is an interesting hole. It can be made tough. It has a small stream running across in front of the green. The green is gorgeous and big. Your tee shot must be accurate as the drive is out of a shoot.

Hole 12
Yards: 321
Handicap: 18
Par: 4

Description: This is a nice hole and a big hitter can drive it. A line of maple trees on the right frames it. It is one of our smaller greens and can be difficult to putt. You really need to read the green very closely. We can make the greens on this hole very slick and very difficult. When driving, stay close to the maples on the right side because the fairway slopes right to left.

Hole 13
Yards: 128
Handicap: 14
Par: 3

Description: This hole has a sloping front and a level back. This hole can be difficult with pin placements. It has a large and elongated green that has a lot of undulation and break to it.

Hole 14
Yards: 290
Handicap: 10
Par: 4

Description: This is one of the favorite short holes. It is featured on the front of our scorecards. The view is beautiful on top of the hill. The green has flat spots. You need to be prepared to place your shots on this green; otherwise your ball can roll off very easily. The best view of the course is from the area around 14. Club selection from the tee is very important. It has an elevated teeing area.

Hole 15
Yards: 418
Handicap: 1
Par: 4

Description: This hole is up on the hill. You go down across a valley and up another slope. It has a large green with terrific positions for pin placements. Woods border the entire left side of the hole. Prevailing winds from the right push many balls left into the woods. It is difficult to birdie and you should put the premium on your second shot. It is a beautiful green and the left 1/3 of the green slopes to the left and away from the tee.

Hole 16
Yards: 369
Handicap: 3
Par: 4

Description: This hole sits right on top of the hill. It is a tough hole to play. There are no out-of-bounds. The green is large and difficult. It is the most severe hole on the golf course. If your second shot does not hit the surface of the green then you are faced with pitching the ball to the green.

Hole 17
Yards: 334
Handicap: 11
Par: 4

Description: A nice drive and a pitch for this hole. It has a small green that you must read well. This is one of the hardest greens to read on the course and the green is very slick.

Hole 18
Yards: 365
Handicap: 12
Par: 4

Description: This is a beautiful finishing hole. It can be made difficult with pin placement to the left. It's a slight dogleg left with your second shot to a slightly elevated green. The left side of the green is like a cavity back that slopes towards the right and the left side of the green will roll severely to the right. It is reasonably easy and very enjoyable hole. The second Crimson maple was planted at this finishing hole in honor and memory of Marcella.

My son Larry has been the superintendent for 29 years. He was mowing fairways when he was 8 and there's not a better golf course superintendent around. In fact, Clearview's green on Hole 15 was featured in the 1998 NASA Annual Report for a hydroponics study on plants to be grown in space on the Mars space mission.

All the holes at Clearview are my favorite since I designed them, but Hole 14 is probably the most unique hole because you can change and move the pin placements around to make it easier or much more difficult. Mark A. Marazza, the club-champion since 1992 says his favorite hole is 15 because he thinks it's the most challenging hole on the course. The club pro, my daughter Renee likes hole 11 from the back tees. Hole 11 is old 9. However, she's partial to the view and specialness of Hole 14. And the course superintendent, my son Larry's favorite hole is number 16 because it is the most difficult green to maintain on the course.

You may wonder how Clearview got its name. I named it Clearview because of the striking clear view from the area of the old 7th tee, now 9. Actually, there's a clear view from most anywhere that you stand on these 130 acres.

Aerial view of Clearview, Christmas 1976

Bill Powell - *Director of Golf*

Lawrence Powell - *Greens Superintendent*

Renee Powell - *Head Golf Professional*

CLUB RULES

1. All players must have a set of clubs.
2. Tee off between markers only - as required by U.S.G.A.
3. Shirts must be worn at all times.
4. Please replace divots and repair ball marks on green.
5. Keep carts off tees and 15 feet from green collars.
6. Balls lying against banks or ditch on entrance road can be moved and dropped to nearest point of relief but not nearer the hole without penalty.
7. U.S.G.A. Rules govern all play not covered by club rules.

CLEARVIEW GOLF CLUB
7 miles east of Canton on Route 30
330-488-0404

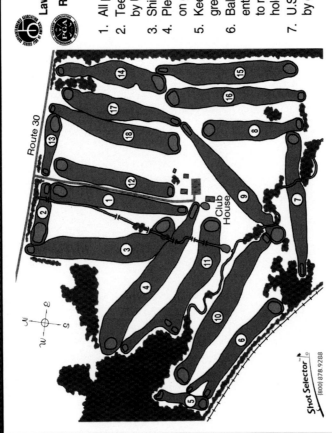

Route 30

Club House

Shot Selector™
(800) 878.9288

Scorer _____

Attest _____   Date _____

Chapter Eight: At Long Last

*"When we stand in defense of our principles
the tides of adversity eventually subside."*

Anonymous

The tides of adversity began to subside in 1988 when I was inducted into the Canton Negro Old Timers Hall of Fame sponsored by the Canton Negro Old Timers Athletic Association. Now, I really didn't consider myself an old timer, yet I was very appreciative of the Hall of Fame honor. Then the tide really turned in 1992, at long last. Our family was nominated and was named the 1992 National Golf Foundation's Jack Nicklaus Golf Family of the Year. We could hardly believe it. The news release from the National Golf Foundation dated August 31, 1992 in part read:

"Former LPGA player, Renee Powell and her family have been selected to receive the National Golf Foundation's Jack Nicklaus Golf Family Award for 1992. The announcement was made by NGF President and CEO, Joseph Beditz. Presented by the NGF since 1986, the award recognizes families who have made substantial contributions to the game and exemplify the ideals of golf and family. It also focuses attention on the role of families in introducing new players to the game. NGF research shows that over 80 percent of all golfers are introduced to the game by family or friends.

The award was created in conjunction with NGF's family golf campaign, which Jack Nicklaus was instrumental in creating in 1985. His name was added to the award in recognition of his interest and early involvement in the NGF's family golf efforts. The Nicklaus family was the first recipient of the award. Others have included the families of Nancy Lopez, Jim Cook, Pat Bradley, Jim Gallagher, and Joe Jemsek.

Powell's playing career began at age three when she learned the game under the tutelage of her father. She entered her first tournament at age 12 - a women's championship at the Seneca Golf Course in Broadview Heights, Ohio - and won. By age 15, she had collected over 30 trophies and was featured in Ebony magazine.

For her, it all began at Clearview. 'This place will always be important to me. It's home - but it's also history. And that's something that my family will always have.'" [8]

This award was deeply significant in so many ways. First, it was gratifying that the National Golf Foundation recognized the Powell family for 46 years of persevering while providing a source of recreation to our community and promoting the game of golf, especially to juniors.

Secondly, it was a personal triumph. One man can stand for what he believes in and have enough might to make it right, especially racial injustice. We won, at long last.

Thirdly, it demonstrated to literally hundreds of nay sayers that I had not just been chasing a dream but actually pursuing and living my dream. All the folks who for decades called me crazy or said down right mean things about Clearview and me had no choice except to realize they had been wrong all these years.

Perhaps most important, this award opened many doors to my 50 year over night success. Interviews, newspaper articles, appearances on television blossomed and began to unfold.

That same year I received the Cornerstone of Freedom Award from the Martin Luther King, Jr. Commission in Canton. In 1995, I was inducted into the Minerva High School Hall of Fame by the Minerva Education Foundation & Alumni Association. I also was named the 1995 Trend Setter in Sports by Gloria Daniels & Associates.

Slowly the tide of recognition was rising. In 1996, I was inducted into the Black Golf Hall of Fame by the National Black Golf Hall of Fame. On May 24, 1996 at a black tie affair, I was honored with the Diamond in the Rough Sports Tribute at Glenmoor Country Club. The featured speaker was Joe Beditz, president and CEO of the National Golf Foundation. His remarks expressed the spirit of the times in 1946 when I was breaking ground on Clearview.

"Most people who make history don't know they are doing it at the time. And like many championship golfers who make it look so easy, Bill Powell and his tremendous commitment made it look easy. But oh, how hard it must have been."

I was wired for sound by CBS-TV sound technician Isadore Bleckman and CBS-TV cameraman Dan Gianneschi explained how the special CBS Sunday crew operates. CBS Sunday was among the media covering the event. The Golf Channel was also filming the tribute and awards dinner.

Dr. Obie Bender, assistant to the president at Baldwin-Wallace College made a special presentation of an official B-W rocking chair.

"In the 150-year tradition of our college, only very special people get one of these," explained Bender. "Among those who have one of these chairs are a former vice president of the United States, a former senator, an astronaut and Olympic Gold Medal winner Harrison Dillard, and now William Powell," said Bender.

I felt honored and thanked some old football-playing friends for showing up, including Cleveland Browns Pro Football Hall of Famer Marion Motley, who was with two other former pro players: Dr. Tony Adamle, Al Jenkins, and Ben Davis.

Hall of Famer Paul Warfield presented my final toast by saying, "He's a great American and a visionary, a risk taker. He was committed to excellence, his children and family, and to his community."

Cindy L. Davis, vice president of the LPGA was there to add her personal and professional congratulations.

"We at the LPGA have admired Bill Powell from a distance through his daughter Renee. There has been a special relationship with Renee as a tour player and a club pro, and it has become perfectly clear where she got all those good and endearing qualities that make her so popular among her fellow professionals," Davis said.

Renee and my sister Mary Alice Walker also participated in the tribute. Marcella was recovering from a recent heart attack and was home under doctor's orders. During all this time, Marcella's health was failing. What a bittersweet time that was as we approached Clearview's 50th anniversary in 1996. Little did any of us know that, sadly, a few short weeks later Marcella would pass away. I still get this gut wrenching feeling in my stomach every time my thoughts turn to the realization that just when we were beginning to receive recognition for 50 years of history in the making, Marcella was not here to share in the honor and kudos.

God must have had a plan because as soon as Marcella got to heaven she obviously got busy. For the newspaper articles, magazine features, television appearances, interviews, book and movie offers began to pour in. I know she has had a guiding hand in Clearview coming into the eye of America and helping those of us left behind to insure that Clearview leaves a clear legacy of triumph over adversity.

My name was popping up everywhere. Sports Illustrated, the International Herald Tribune, Golf Market Today, Golf Magazine, Industry, Club & Course Management, Golf World, Golf Course Management, the Beacon Journal, USA Today, PGA Magazine, the Canton Respository, People Magazine, ProReport, The Limbaugh Letter, Ohio Magazine, Ebony Magazine, and the Chicago Tribune to mention a few.

When I appeared on the front page of the New York Times on Friday, June 28, 1996 I had the feeling I was definitely going to get noticed. Congratulatory letters started to pour in from individuals and CEOs to legislators and golf professionals. I didn't mind all of the accolades but that certainly isn't why I built Clearview.

More honors followed. I received a special proclamation and personal congratulations from the then Governor of the state of Ohio now U.S. Senator, George V. Voinovich. I also received a lifetime of achievement citation from the Senate of the 123rd General Assembly of Ohio signed by Senator Richard H. Finan, President of the Ohio Senate and Senator Dick Schafrath from the 19th Senatorial District.

Year '97 proved to be a landmark year as well. In the March issue of *Reader's Digest* they featured my life story in their "Heroes For Today" article titled "The Right Course."

As if miracles would not cease, I was advised in writing in November of 1997, that I had been awarded an Honorary PGA membership, by the PGA of America, Northern Ohio Section. The day I received the letter notifying me of my honorary PGA membership was a day I will never forget. After all this time, after my attempts to join the PGA in the early 1960s, now, at long last, I was finally going to become a member of the organization that I had dreamed about belonging to. I not only had to blink twice and re-read the letter, I had to pinch myself as well.

By this time my story had been told around the world on television programs such as CBS Sunday Morning, Day and Date, Extra, The Gordon Elliott Show, Fast Forward, and MSNBC.

In 1998, I received the "First" Legend of Golf Award by the Woodholme Foundation and induction into the Ohio Veterans Hall of Fame. In February, *Guideposts* featured my life story in a four-page article titled: "I'll Just Build My Own." Interestingly, one of their quotes appeared at the end of the article that hopefully gave every reader pause for thought:

"Watch your thoughts; they become words. Watch your words; they become actions. Watch your actions;

they become habits. Watch your habits; they become your character. Watch your character; it becomes your destiny." - Frank Outlaw. [9]

Guideposts Magazine has a circulation of millions around the world and I was amazed at the response to the article. People wrote to me from all points across the globe. They were touched, inspired, and motivated. People seemed to need to know that no matter what their situations are, there is hope and that we not only should but must turn hate into love and bitterness into joy. This is a strong message we all need to understand.

A very special accolade came from the Tiger Woods Foundation by naming their annual scholarship awards the William and Marcella Powell Scholarships. The Tiger Woods Foundation is a charitable organization founded in 1996 by Tiger and his father, Earl Woods. The humanitarian foundation strives for a world where people of varying background, histories, races, languages and ethnicity can all reach their highest potential and participate fully in the economic mainstream of society. It supports programs that focus on creating positive environments for underprivileged youth and emphasizes the importance of parental involvement and responsibility in the lives of children.

One of my most spectacular shining moments happened on June 12, 1998 when I received an honorary degree of Doctor of Humane Letters from Baldwin-Wallace College in Berea, Ohio. President Neal Malicky humbled me in his citation:

"Distinguished dreamer, faithful follower of your convictions, tireless worker, and outstanding human being, Baldwin-Wallace College salutes you and welcomes you to the ranks of her honorary alumni.

Your perseverance toward your goal is inspiring. In 1946, you returned to your home in Canton, having served four years overseas with the Army Air Corps. Having played golf on many courses in Europe, you pursued your passion for the game at a public course in your hometown where you were made to feel unwelcome.

Undaunted, you decided to build your own golf course. With the unwavering support of your wife Marcella, you found the land for your project. Unable to secure a G.I. Loan, despite being a veteran and long-time employee at the Timken Roller Bearing Company, you finally received the financial backing from family and friends.

You designed and constructed the course yourself and, in 1948, opened the nine-hole Clearview Golf Course, the first golf course in America owned and designed by an African American, where all were welcome and no one was turned away because of their race. Despite some vandalism and ill will, you prevailed and overcame the prejudices of those who sought to discourage your dream. With the aid of your family, you maintained the golf course, while continuing your night-shift job to repay those who had backed you. In the 1970s you expanded Clearview to an 18-hole course.

Your dedication and commitment served as a model for your children. Your son Larry serves as the superintendent of Clearview. Your daughter Renee, one of only three African American women to ever play on the LPGA Tour, is currently the Clearview golf pro. The Powell family is among a very small group to receive the National Golf Foundation's highest award, the prestigious Jack Nicklaus Award, which honors the year's outstanding golf family in the United States.

William Powell, for your commitment to your beliefs, your steadfast work ethic and your dedication to your dream of an inclusive society with equal opportunities for all Americans, Baldwin-Wallace College salutes you and is proud to confer upon you today the honorary degree of Doctor of Humane Letters."

At the private reception for my honorary degree I was blessed to have Edie Jones, a dear and loyal friend since childhood at my side. Edie's been there through it all. We first met as children when I was peddling newspapers to her parent's house. Then we began walking to school together. We shared a close and special friendship and had a lot in common, mainly athletics. Edie was very athletic and involved in every sport offered like I was. She won letters in every sport she played. After finishing high school together in Minerva Edie went on to spend two years at Kent State University. She joined the Army for four years during the war and stayed in the reserves and came out a Captain. She was a warrant officer during the war. She spent only one month assigned to Ft. Des Moines in Iowa and was one of only six women sent in to the Chief of Staff's office in Washington, D.C. Her assignment in Washington was Assistant in the Office of the Chief of Staff to the Commander in Chief, William D. Leahy. After her military career she went to Miami University to finish her bachelor's degree and obtain her masters degree. She became the Dean of Students in Montana and after a few years went to the University of Washington in

Seattle on a Ford Foundation Scholarship. She must have missed all of us because she came back east and became the principal scientist at the American Institutes for Research in the field of ergonomics for developing countries and the upper atmosphere. Edie and three other research scientists then formed their own research firm. Our childhood friendship bridged the decades and we always remained in close touch with each other and our families. In fact, Edie is only one of three individuals who have a lifetime membership at Clearview Golf Club and she's had it for a long time. A true friend she has been, indeed.

My sister Mary Alice, my daughter Renee and my son Larry were right there by my side as well. Family members that traveled distances to share in this victory and celebration included Norman and Helen Hill and Ron and Rose Marie Hill

A special family friend, Ellen Nösner, was also there. At one point during the reception at the Alumni House she was in the foyer moving from the living room to the dining room. As she entered the foyer, she noticed the front door opening very slowly as if someone invisible was entering. She felt an instant chill and immediately sensed it must be Marcella. As soon as the door had gently opened it gently began to close under its own mysterious power.

Ellen came to me right away and whispered in my ear, "Dr. P., Marcella just arrived. She's here with you to celebrate this joyous occasion."

It did seem that at long last I had come full circle in this life, and it was comforting and a blessing to know that Marcella was still by my side after all.

Dr. Powell, June 12th, 1998

Bride and groom at 50 years

Chapter Nine: Full Circle

"To Dr. William J. Powell...
your appearance on national television
was an inspiration to me and my 13-year-old son.
Thank you for never giving up
and contributing so much to society."

Dan Lindemann
Pensacola, Florida

Becoming a Life Member of the PGA of America in 1999 was full circle. The circle widened with the PGA of America's landmark announcement in August of 1999 at the PGA Championship Tournament at Medina Country Club in Chicago, Illinois. The press release titled "PGA Leads Renovation of Historic Clearview Golf Club" in part stated, "The PGA of America is leading the renovation of Clearview Golf Club in East Canton, Ohio the first and only golf course in the United States designed, built, owned, and managed by an African American.

The project begins this fall, and Clearview will celebrate its re-grand opening in spring 2001 with a celebrity golf tournament and festivities. One of the goals is to register the property as a historic designated landmark.

Dr. William J. Powell, founder and owner of Clearview Golf Club, began building his plans for a new course in the 1940s, a time when African Americans had limited access to golf facilities. As a result he created his own place to play and opened the first nine holes of Clearview in 1948 on what used to be a dairy farm.

Today, two of his children are actively involved in the day-to-day operations. Daughter Renee, who spent 13 years on the LPGA Tour, is Head PGA Professional at Clearview. Ms. Powell also runs the Renee Powell Youth Golf Program for urban youth in Cleveland. Son Lawrence, a member of the Golf Course Superintendents Association of America, is Clearview's course superintendent. The course is located in the Northern Ohio PGA Section of the PGA of America, which awarded Dr. Powell an honorary PGA membership in March 1997.

"The PGA of America is pleased to be involved with Clearview because of the property's historical and cultural significance," said PGA President Will Mann. "Clearview and the Powell family are inspirational examples of entrepreneurship in the golf business. We hope the perpetuation of the Clearview and Powell legacy will inspire future generations."

The proposed renovations will update the 130-acre property to make it compatible with traditional golf courses. The redesign of two greens and two holes will lengthen the 18-hole course from its current 5,800 yards to 6,300 yards. The practice and teeing areas will be leveled and enlarged. The creation of a 1.4-acre lake will support a new irrigation system. The clubhouse and golf shop will be renovated, and the restroom and locker rooms will be modernized. New maintenance and storage facilities will be built. Other improvements include replacing directional signage to the property and widening the entrance roads to allow two lanes of traffic instead of the current one.

To offset construction costs, the PGA is negotiating with corporate partners in the golf industry to donate materials and services to the project.

The PGA has enlisted the support of Dr. Michael Hurdzan and Pete Dye, well-known golf course architects, to work closely with the Powell family to oversee Clearview's renovation.

The Clearview Golf Club renovation is one of many programs the PGA of America supports in its ongoing efforts to make the game of golf fun and accessible for people of any ability, gender, or race. National programs such as PGA Golf in Schools, Clubs for Kids and Kids in Course reach thousands of African American youths each year. The PGA is also involved with organizations such as the National Minority Junior Golf Scholarship Association, National Black College Golf Coaches' Association, National Police Athletic League, National Collegiate Athletic Association, National Youth Sports Program, and the Renee Powell Youth Golf Program. In addition, The PGA hosts and operates the National Minority College Golf Championship held at the PGA Golf Club at PGA Village in Port St. Lucie, Florida." [10]

This announcement represented the quintessence of equality to me. To go full circle from not being welcome on golf courses in the 1940s, to being denied membership in the professional association of which I had every right to be a member, to having to build my own golf course on a prayer and a dream, to having the PGA of America admit me as a Lifetime member, to the PGA of America recognizing the historical and cultural legacy that Clearview represents in America is far more than gratifying. It clearly demonstrates that Clearview is America's course. Together, the PGA of America and

Clearview Golf Club and the Powell family will leave a legacy for this generation and all those following, that states we were committed working together to demonstrate that inclusiveness, equality, entrepreneurship and inspiration is a worthy legacy for us to carry into the future. All of this is being created through the love of the game! Quite a testament for getting to the course on a regular basis, I'd say.

Well, the renovation project is underway. Dr. Michael Hurdzan completed the blueprint design of the renovated course. During the winter of 1999, the west portion of the course was prepared for additional yardage area. Although there have been delays I am hopeful the course will be ready for its re-grand opening in spring of 2001. Then the circle will truly be strong enough to embrace all of society no matter what their ability, gender, or race. That should give us all hope.

I received the news that Ohio Congresswoman Stephanie Tubbs Jones, the first African American congresswoman from the state of Ohio, had nominated me as the recipient of the Congressional Black Caucus First Annual Unsung Hero Award. The award was presented in Washington, D.C. and its purpose is to recognize those individuals who have made significant contributions to society in the areas of business, sports, the arts, and community social change. It was a moving and meaningful ceremony. It was a full circle defining moment. To think that a black man was being honored and had been selected by his congressional representative and in my case it was a black woman, the first in the state of Ohio. Praise the Lord!

October 1999 was a powerful month. On

October 4, I was a national panelist at the Smithsonian in Washington, D.C. on African Americans and the Game of Golf: Past, Present, and Future. What a moment. Especially since I shared the stage with my daughter Renee.

The publicity for the event appeared in The Smithsonian Associate and was described as, "Although there are written accounts of African American athletes participating in many professional sports, little has been published about the involvement of African Americans in the game of golf. Hear a distinguished panel discuss significant personalities and events pertaining to African Americans and golf, as they share personal recollections of attempts to break the racial and gender barriers of the game. They also comment on the future of African Americans in the sport. Panelists include Pete McDaniel, Golf Digest senior writer; Calvin H. Sinnette, golf historian and author; Renee Powell, veteran LPGA player and first African American female to earn a PGA Class "A" membership; William Powell, sole African American 18-hole golf course designer, builder, owner, and operator; William Dickey, founder, National Minority Junior Golf Scholarship Association; and Craig Bowen, executive director, National Minority College Golf Scholarship Fund."[11]

That event was history in the making. My only regret is that the panel discussion was not video taped because it was lively, historical, honest and hopeful. We need to constantly, at every opportunity, be open about the past, forgive it and heal, and move on to a hopeful future where the world will be different because we have made it so. That is our duty.

I'd like to tell you about a man who does what he believes and knows what he must do to build a better world. In November 1998, my daughter Renee who is a consultant for the First Tee program was a speaker at their first annual meeting at the World Golf Village in St. Augustine, Florida. I was in the audience. So was Mr. Fred T. Tattersall.

I met him the day of the presentation and the next morning he went into the office of Todd Leiweke and said he was going to write a $1,000,000 check to endow The First Tee program. His intent and purpose of his gift was that the money be used for a scholarship program to honor Dr. William Powell for the Life Skills Program of The First Tee.

The following October at the First Tee Annual Meeting in Houston, Texas Fred presented the check to me on stage. I then turned the check over to Todd Leiweke, Executive Director of The First Tee Program, with a smile on my face. What an unforgettable moment that was for me. A double full circle. A hole-in-one in terms of golf!

Now both the Tiger Woods Foundation and the First Tee program had scholarships directly targeted for youth in honor of me. I never in my wildest dreams would have imagined such a giant step while I was pulling fence posts or seeding Clearview by hand. When you stop and think about how far you've actually come, just by putting one foot in front of the other and never stopping, it is amazing to think what you and I can accomplish.

Fred was kind enough to frame the original million-dollar cashed check on a plaque, which hangs on the west wall of Clearview's clubhouse. In his letter he expresses that he is looking forward to working with me in recognizing kids from across the United States for their leadership and golf skills in summer of 2000, at Kansas State University for the First Tee Life Skills Camp at the Earl Woods National Youth Academy at Kansas State University July 22-29, 2000.

Another of my special moments was opening the invitation I received from Jim Awtrey, CEO of The PGA of America to attend the 1997 Masters Tournament in Augusta, Georgia as his special guest. My LPGA/PGA daughter accompanied me. I, of course, had never been there and what a thrill of a lifetime to actually be there during the tournament. The best part of it all was that the year I was there Tiger Woods became the Master's champion.

Well I've never seen a more beautiful sight than when he and his father embraced as he came off of Hole #18. Tiger has made a quantum jump for the sport of golf and in the process breaking every barrier in this path. Tiger has transcended generational impact influencing the past, present, and the future all at the same time. What serendipity that Nike is the Greek goddess of victory. Tiger is a victor for all times.

Victory prevailed again with my membership election to the Quarter Century Club of the Professional Golfers' Association of America. This award goes to a distinctive group of members who have served golf loyally for twenty-five years or longer.

In November 1999, I spoke at The PGA Annual Meeting in Anaheim, California. The entire 400-member body of the organization was in attendance and after my presentation I was formally awarded and accepted my Lifetime Membership in The PGA of America.

This grand circle would not be complete without acknowledging the great personal sacrifices my family made for Clearview and me. Marcella was my wife and partner and as adults we agreed and knew, at least thought we knew, what we were getting ourselves into. Our children were different. They did not have the opportunity for consent. They were born into it. The consequence of that meant they have made the deepest personal sacrifices of all.

Billy, born William Berry, was the first-born grandchild of my parents. As so often happens he had to be a big brother to both Renee and Larry. The war took me away from him for three years at the most impressionable and formative time in his early young life.

Billy began helping me do the day-in and day-out work at Clearview at a very young age. He was the oldest, he was a boy, and as I look back I believe my dream put untold pressure on him to succeed. In reflection, I now know he was more like me than I ever realized - - strong, determined, fiercely independent, and full of dreams, his own dreams and goals, perhaps too big for my shadow.

Even when Billy went to college at Central State he would come home on the weekends to help me at Clearview. While Billy was in college he met Jim Mitchum, movie actor Robert Mitchum's son, who was attending Antioch College in Yellow Springs, Ohio. That friendship introduced him to many high profile movie and singing stars like Barbra Streisand, Peter, Paul, and Mary, and a managing position with Jose Feliciano. That took him to California.

The 60s were a hard time for all young people, especially young people of color. How he must have struggled. It was a revolutionary and dangerous time for our youth. Some survived and some did not. Billy was one of those casualties. In 1967, in the San Francisco Bay area he was found murdered. That is a tragedy that has scarred our hearts. We have missed Billy every day since. He was a free-spirited soul filled with passion. His gift to us was himself. Life with Billy was a present we cherish along with his memory.

From the very beginning, Renee was a Daddy's girl, and she will always be a Daddy's girl. She took an interest in golf very early. At age three she was swinging with a small driver a golf equipment salesman brought by and a putter that I had cut down for her.

She has always been so much like her mother. Making sure everybody in the family was happy was important to her. It still is. She is beautiful, simply beautiful. That is the one word that describes every aspect of her being.

She spills over with talent in everything she touches, not to mention the fact she is a world-class golfer. Believe me, she has her own story to tell from a different generation and a different gender.

Her interests throughout her golfing career have always been targeted toward youth and women. She is their best advocate. Renee gives the voiceless a voice - - a strong and powerful voice. Her contributions and achievements in all areas stand on their own. I am the proudest father in this world, and the next, of what she has done, is doing, and will continue to do for the sport of golf. Renee is my beautiful little girl.

Marcella had a difficult pregnancy with Lawrence Roger. We almost lost him. She had to stay in bed for weeks. And it is Larry who has perhaps made more personal sacrifices than any of my children, especially after Billy's death. He became a man very quickly and picked up a huge share of the load at Clearview. As a youngster, if he wasn't in school or studying, he was working the course.

No one had to tell Larry to study. He was a brilliant student with straight A's. He has always worked so hard. Perhaps that's what has made him so serious about life. Larry is very focused, a tremendously deep thinker, a man who takes everything to heart, and is the strongest current in any stream.

Since school, he has worked a full-time job in addition to his full-time job at Clearview since college. Larry attended Walsh College, a local Catholic college in Canton. His commitment and dedication to Clearview have eclipsed the pursuit of his own dreams. Instead, he has spent his life tending to my dream. Larry is so brilliant he could have been anything he would have aspired to be...lawyer or brain surgeon or anything in between

He is without question one of the finest golf course superintendents in the nation. Highly respected by his peers. I'm not just saying that as his father. He truly is the best. And I owe him a debt I can never repay, except with my love.

The poet Kahlil Gibran speaks of children in a tender and universal way. "And a woman who held a babe against her bosom said, 'Speak to us of Children.' And he said, 'Your children are not your children. They are the sons and daughters of Life's longing for itself. They come through you but not from you, and though they are with you yet they belong not to you. You may give them your love but not your thoughts, for they have their own thoughts. You may house their bodies but not their souls, for their souls dwell in the house of tomorrow, which you cannot visit, not even in your dreams. You may strive to be like them, but seek not to make them like you. For life goes not backward nor tarries with yesterday. You are the bows from which your children as living arrows are sent forth. The archer sees the mark upon the path of the infinite, and He bends you with His might that His arrows may go swift and far. Let your bending in the archer's hand be for gladness; for even as He loves the arrow that flies, so He loves also the bow that is stable.'" [12]

I confess, my children are my arrows; they represent my full circle. The aim is true. True in my heart.

Larry, 1961 Clearview Open Junior Champ

Billy, 1959 Clearview Club Champion, with Renee

Chapter Ten: The Legacy

"Every few hundred years throughout Western history, a sharp transformation has occurred. In a matter of decades, society altogether rearranges itself-its worldview, its basic values, its social and political structure, its arts, and its key institutions. Fifty years later a New World exists. And the people born into that world cannot even imagine the world in which their own grandparents were born. Our age is in such a period of transformation. If history is any guide, this transformation will not be completed until 2010 or 2020." [13]

Peter Drucker

I believe we are in a period of transition and I pray the outcome will be healing. Hopefully the healing of our society's wounds will crumble the barriers that have been created between us so we can finally come together as one nation and as one people. Clearview is a testament to that transition.

Before 1992, Clearview was not on the tip of everyone's tongue. That year was a turning point. When Clearview is registered as an historic landmark we will be guaranteed that the legacy of America's course will be protected and preserved. I feel peaceful and soothed to know Clearview will endure beyond my time here with you. I am content knowing that the dream I dreamed came true.

That, however, is not enough. Our responsibility is to our youth and from my perspective, the game of golf. Did you know that less than 2% of kids age 12 - 17 are introduced to golf? Did you know that only 3% of golfers are African American? Did you know only 2% of golfers are Hispanic? Did you know the average

age of the beginning golfer is 29? Did you know that most growth in golf over the last 10 years came from households making more than $50,000? [14]

When you consider what George Bush has to say about the game, it is time we position ourselves to support youth all across this country from every walk of life.

He says, "Golf is unique in the values it teaches. A game of honor, integrity and sportsmanship. Golf is governed by the players themselves, who by sticking to the spirit and disciplines of the game, gain the personal fulfillment of pride, self-esteem and self-discipline." [15]

President George Bush is the Honorary Chairman of The First Tee Program that offers a solution to the disparity that exists in our world today.

The First Tee is an initiative to create new facilities and access to golf with a special emphasis on kids who otherwise may not have an opportunity to experience the game.

The true value of the program is based on golf's unique ability to instill and nurture essential values such as honesty, integrity, sportsmanship, and a solid work ethic in young people who are introduced to the game.

The First Tee initiative has the support and participation of a variety of key sectors:
— The leading U.S. golf organizations including the PGA TOUR, United States Golf Association, PGA of America, Ladies Professional Golf Association, and Augusta National Golf Club.
— A wide range of public sector constituencies, including the U.S. Department of Housing and Urban Development, National Recreation and Park Association,

National League of Cities, U.S. Conference of Mayors and the National Association of County Officials.

— A variety of groups, including the Golf Course Superintendents Association of America, National Golf Foundation, American Junior Golf Association, American Society of Golf Course Architects, Tiger Woods Foundation, and National Minority Golf Foundation dedicated to extending the reach of golf to new segments of the population.

When PGA Tour commissioner Tim Finchem introduced The First Tee in November 1997, with the backing of the World Golf Foundation, it represented an unprecedented alliance of golf's major groups. There were skeptics, for sure, who wondered whether the politics of golf's various local and national groups could coexist to make the initiative a success, put aside differences, and work together.

Thankfully, since the introduction of The First Tee, a little more than two years ago, the concept has taken off. It's giving children a better chance to play golf and is creating affordable and accessible opportunities, particularly for minority children who traditionally haven't had access to golf.

That is why it is a perfect platform for me to endorse and support the heart of their objectives:

- Improve the game's accessibility, making golf more available to people of all social strata particularly children.
- Provide every child, regardless of race and economic background the opportunity to learn and play golf.
- Instill the game's inherently positive values.

- Teach children that dedication, sound values, and education are keys to success.
- Develop in participants greater self-esteem, civic responsibility, and greater confidence to broaden their goals in life.
- Create employment and advanced educational opportunities for participants.

These objectives should be our legacy.

The goal of First Tee organizers was to have 100 First Tee chapters/facilities in some stage of production by the end of its third year in 2000, and a long-term goal of 1,000. The number of First Tee chapters in North America has nearly tripled in the past year, growing from 25 to 87 chapters under some form of contract. There are approximately 180 communities interested in establishing First Tee chapters.

July 2000 is the inaugural First Tee Leadership Camp at Kansas State University at the newly formed Earl Woods National Youth Academy. The camp will be an annual event for two children from each of the First Tee facilities for a weeklong mentoring and leadership camp. I will be there and so will Fred Tattersall of the Richmond, Virginia First Tee chapter who endowed the camp for life by donating $1 million to create the Dr. William Powell Scholarships, which are earmarked for the camp. Dr. Steve Danish, the pioneer sports psychologist for the program, who has done extensive work in developing a sports/leadership curriculum for the camp, is also attending.

Getting the First Tee chapter started in Richmond, Virginia hasn't been easy for Fred. For more than a year, some Richmond residents vehemently opposed his proposed minority-focused facility. But he forged ahead. Fred is a successful white businessman who recognized that no was not the right answer. He is now only months away from unveiling The First Tee's first new 18-hole facility.

Tattersall predicts The First Tee's legacy will be more than golf, particularly since life skills have been adopted into the First Tee curriculum. "I think what started out as a good project to introduce golf to kids who otherwise wouldn't have the opportunity to play, has expanded beyond the idea of just teaching golf," Tattersall said. "That's the big change I see happening at the local and national level. Do we just want to create 100,000 more junior golfers to be eventual adult golfers one day, or stronger families and better values in kids? I think we'll see both because we think the sport of golf has those attributes. With the right mentors, we can impact quite a few kids." [16]

So, if you are an adult, the question becomes, to whom are you a mentor? We must collectively agree not to fail our children. If we want the future to be better, we better be focusing and taking positive action toward our youth, not just thinking or talking about it.

Clearly, Fred Tattersall is a leader who takes mentoring quite serious. There are many more and I ask, "Would you step forward?" We need you.

Clearview is more than a golf course. It is a blueprint that teaches young and old dreaming dreams is not whimsical. It's essential. I still have dreams to dream and things to do.

As Peter Drucker predicts, we are in the process of a sharp transformation. This is an era of dynamic opportunity to lovingly impact our children from the ground up. Consider what we create when we take time to recreate with our nation's children. If it's true that to dream is to create the future, let's dream a future full of loving choices for our children.

To those of you who are young readers, you must find a mentor. Find a mentor where you can light on their wings so they can help you fly. Find someone who will listen to you - - understand you - - encourage you. A mentor relationship will help you grow, excel, and achieve. If it is not a parent, find an aunt or an uncle, a family friend, a librarian, a teacher...just find someone who is willing to help you see your potential. If someone turns you down do not fall into despair. Try someone else.

You can also remind them of the words of Rabbi Hillel who said, "If not us, who? If not now, when? If I am not for myself who will be for me, but if I am only for myself what am I?" [17]

You may find comfort in the Latin words that hung on a plaque above the world famous psychologist Carl Jung's home in Switzerland. They are also carved on his tombstone. These words will remind you we are never alone.

"Vocatus atque non, Vocatus deus aderit." [18]
Translated it says, "Whether invoked or not, God is present."

May God's presence bless you in the pursuit of your dreams.

My story is now yours. My soul is now unbound. May the struggle and triumph of my life wrap itself around you with a healing and understanding that sends the message to forgive and move on. Don't dwell on the past. Be present now. Write on your heart that hope triumphs over bitterness, and love conquers hate.

Believe in yourself even if no one else does. Never let anyone or anything stand in your way of accomplishing something for the greater good. Stand firm. Stand tall. Never give up and never give in.

My course - it's a clear view (1997)

I Am

Appendix

Wetland Report for Clearview Golf Course

In a recent Wetland Delineation report for the Clearview Golf Course, Dr. Andrew M. White, President of Environmental Resource Associates, Inc., provided a concise site location and description.

In part it states, "The site known as the Clearview Golf Course parcel is located within Osnaburg Township, Stark County, Ohio. It contains an existing golf course, narrow strips of trees adjacent to existing fairways, and a small tract of undeveloped contiguous land in the northwest portion of the parcel. A second area, southwest of the N&W Railroad tracks, is inaccessible from the existing golf course and also remains undeveloped.

The northern boundary of the Clearview Golf Course property is adjacent to U.S. Route 30. The entrance driveway into the golf course is approximately 1,130 feet to the clubhouse. From the driveway the parcel boundary continues east along U.S. 30 for 900 feet. The property line then turns south for approximately 2,200 feet to the southeast corner.

The southern property line then moves 2,730 feet to the west, turns north for 1,870 feet jogs 1,150 feet east and continues northeast for a remaining 675 feet to the northwestern corner. The boundary then extends approximately 630 feet east, parallel to U.S. 30, to the entrance drive.

Within the golf course property the USGS topographic mappings (composite of East Canton and Robertsville quadrangles) show one man-made ditch and an unnamed intermittent tributary of Little Sandy Creek. No wetlands, marshes, or lakes are indicated. The man-made ditch (flowing north to south) has previously been channeled and passes between existing fairways and the entrance drive. The intermittent stream is partially within the undeveloped portion of the parcel in the northwest. Elsewhere, the stream is bordered by the well-manicured fairways of the existing golf course.

The USFWS National Wetlands Inventory mapping (1977) marks an area in the west-central portion of the site as PEMY [19] (see glossary) . This area is and has been developed into the fairways, greens, and tees of the course for more than 50 years." [20]

Endnotes

[1] Henry Wadsworth Longfellow "Longfellows Poetical Works, subtitled: Poems by Henry Wadsworth Longfellow", 4th Edition, Philadelphia, Carey & Hart, 1846. Entered according to act of Congress in the year 1845 by Carey & Hart in the Clerks office of the District Court of the eastern district of Pennsylvania.

[2] "Complete Works of Emily Dickinson", Little Brown & Co. of Toronto & Boston, ©1960, 714, number 1765.

[3.] Gibran, Kahlil, "The Prophet", published by Alfred A. Knopf, Inc., 125th printing, April 1994.

[4.] Emerson, Ralph Waldo. Source: www.gurlpages.com/nolabel/you_know_who13/quotes.html.

[5] "Queen Mary (Superliner Pictorial)", ©1997, all rights reserved. Graphic Design and Text by J. Bryce Gillespie; pg. 6 (fact capsule).

[6.] D. Combs, "Dreams Come True", Our Card Collection.

[7] Foss, Samual Walter. Source: www.ipoet.com/archive/original/foss/house.html. See full poem on page 147.

[8] Bill Burbaum and Trish Davis ,. "Renee Powell Family Selected for 1992 Jack Nicklaus Golf Family Award" August 31, 1992, for immediate release, Jupiter, FL.

[9.] Guidepost, February 1998, 9.

[10] PGA Golf Marketing, Sept. 2, 1999.

[11] Smithsonian Associate by the Smithsonian Institution, October 1999, 6- 7.

[12] Gibran, Kahlil, "The Prophet", published by Alfred A. Knopf, Inc., 125th printing, April 1994, 17-18.

[13.] Drucker, Peter, FOCUS newsletter, "On Child Welfare in Ohio", Jan 2000.

[14] First Tee Brochure, April, 1999, as provided by the National Golf Foundation.

[15] Ibid.

[16] 25th Anniversary edition of Golf Week, "Initiative Aims for Greater Golf Access" April 10, 2000, 36.

[17] Pirke, "Chapter Avot, Chapters of the Fathers", Chapter 1: Mishnah 14. As translated by Mr. Phil Cohen, Hillel Jewish Student Center.

[18] Robert & Mary Collison/Facts of File Publisher, Dictionary of Foreign Quotations, NY, NY, ©1980, 139.

[19] per Richard A. Wolinski, Environmental Quality Anaylst; Lakes and Wetlands, Dept. of Environmental Quality.

[20] White, Andrew M., Ph.D, Environmental Resource Associates, Inc. "Wetland Delineation for the Clearview Golf Course Parcel, Osnaburg Township, East Canton, Ohio," Nov. 15, 1999. Report 050-232.

Glossary

35-knots - a knot is a unit of speed; one nautical mile per hour. 35 knots equals 35 nautical miles per hour.

35-mm shot - size of a shot made for a 35-mm gun.

anti-aircraft guns, 105's - ground based guns that shot at aircraft.

bivouack - a temporary encampment often in the open air.

D-Day - June 6, 1944, when allied forces landed on the beach in Normandy, France during WWII, also used as a code name during any war.

fox hole - a hole in the ground that soldiers dig for protection. Good protection except with direct hit.

Jim Crow Car - the first car in back of the steam engine; Jim Crow was the subject of a song in the 19th century becoming a discriminatory term for the treatment of people of color.

Ku Klux Klan - A secret society organized in the south after the Civil War to reassert white supremacy with terroristic methods.

Nazis - a member of the National Socialist German Worker's Party, founded in Germany in 1919 and brought to power in 1933 under Adolf Hitler.

PEMY - P = Palustrine (a marshy area with standing water, often associated with a stream), EM = emergent, Y = saturated, semipermanent, seasonal.

Shrapnel - the leavings of a shell that has fallen to earth.

SS Troops - the elite Nazi-fighting men.

VJ Day - Victory over Japan.

WAC's - Womens Army Corp.

Golf Terms

Annual Concrete Tournament - Annual Louis Petros & Sons Scramble hosted by Louis Petros & Sons concrete company.

Bobby Jones - only amateur to win the grand slam.

Bristol Steel - type of steel that started to be used after hickory shaft.

bunker, trap shot - hazard consisting of a prepared area of ground with sand in it. Also called a sand trap.

caddy - one hired to serve as an attendant to a golfer, especially by carrying the golf clubs.

caddy master - supervisor of all caddies.

Club Car - name of company that supplies golf cars.

golf clubs: woods: 1, 3, 5, 7 - woods are used for driving from the tee.
                         irons: 3, 4, 5, 6, 7, 8, 9 - irons are used for fairway and hazard shots.
                         pitching wedge - a wedge used to loft the golf ball over objects.
                         sand wedge - a wedge used to get the golf ball out of sand traps.
                         putter - a short golf club used for putting.

In general the lower numbers are for distance and the higher the number the greater the loft of the ball.

Grand Slam - made up of four amateur golf tournaments: British Open, British Amateur Open, U.S. Open and U.S. Amateur Open.

Hagen Iron - trade name after golfer Walter Hagen.

LPGA - Ladies Professional Golf Association.

Niblick - a 9 iron.

Open up the face of the club and cut the shot - sitting the face of the club in such a way as to add more loft and swinging the golf club on an outside to inside plane.

PGA - Professional Golf Association.

Red chewing fescue, highland bent grass, Astoria bent grass, Pencross, Lofts-93, A-6 bent grass, poa - different types of cool weather grasses.

shaft - part of the club between the grip and the head.

stimpmeter - a device developed by the USGA to measure the speed of greens.

Timothy rough - thick high grass.

wedge club - club design with more than the 9 iron loft and has a flange on the bottom.

Clearview

Photo Gallery

Mr. P and Willie Green of the Miami Dolphins

With all my love darling, "Muzzy"

Love and kisses, your Bill

Officer Berry Powell

Mr. P, a fine man at 21

1992 National Golf Foundation's Jack Nicklaus Family of the Year

Mr. P newly pinned with PGA Lifetime Membership pin poses with daughter Renee and Ryder Cup trophy (November 1999)

LPGA/PGA and Clearview Club Pro Renee Powell

Mr. P and life long friend Euley Glenn

Mr. P and Mr. Fred Tattersall

Mr. P with Senator Gene Watts presenting his Ohio Veterans Hall of Fame plaque

Mr. P and Hank Aaron at 1st Renee Powell/Anheuser Busch Celebrity Golf Tournament

Clearview Special Events

- Annual Renee Powell Pro-Am - takes place in June each year to benefit the Ronald McDonald House Charities and the Ohio Special Olympics.
- Annual Renee Powell/Anheuser Busch Celebrity Tournament - held each year on the last Saturday in August this tournament gives amateur players a chance to play golf with current NFL, NBA and other major sports players. Proceeds benefit the United Negro College Fund.
- The Marcella Powell Memorial Clearview Women's Open Tournament - takes place each September and allows women golfers to pit their talents against one another.

For more information about special events
and club logo items contact us at:
(330) 488-0404

We are located 2 miles east of East Canton on U.S. Route 30.
8410 Lincoln Street
P.O. Box 30196
East Canton, OH 44730

See our website at: www.Clearview-gc.com